THE GROTTO MAKERS

THE GROTTO MAKERS

Joseph and Josiah Lane of Tisbury

CHRISTINA RICHARD

First published in the United Kingdom in 2018

by The Hobnob Press,
8 Lock Warehouse, Severn Road, Gloucester GL1 2GA
www.hobnobpress.co.uk

British Library Cataloguing in Publication Data
A catalogue record for this book is available from the British Library

ISBN 978-1-906978-54-9

Typeset in Scala.
Typesetting and origination by John Chandler

Printed by Lightning Source

The cover design incorporates a photograph of 'Seated Man 2011', a sculpture by Sean Henry in front of Place Farm Barn, Tisbury (by kind permission of Messums Wiltshire).

CONTENTS

ACKNOWLEDGEMENTS AND THANKS

I have been helped by a number of people whilst I have been writing this book, and I would like to thank the following:

The staff at Wiltshire & Swindon History Centre at Chippenham and Tisbury History Society for the use of the Archive facilities.

At Fonthill, Lord Margadale, Simon Fowler and John D'Arcy. At Claremont, the National Trust Property Administrator, Kim Kitson, and at Belcombe Court, the staff including the gardeners. Catherine Burchall was helpful at Wimborne St Giles, and Cherrill Sands at Painshill. In particular Julia Mottershaw at Stourhead was enthusiastic and encouraging, as was Mike Cousins, allowing me to have copies of his various grotto researches. Mr and Mrs Douglas of Duntish Court (CastleHill) were very kind and welcoming.

Caroline Dakers and Liz Curzen were kind enough to read the manuscript and make suggestions. In Tisbury Alan Frame helped work out the geography of the properties in Hindon Lane, and Phil Chapman made sense of the Lane family tree from my scribbled sheet.

Most importantly thanks to John Chandler of the Hobnob Press, who had enough faith to publish the book.

Finally, thanks to Mike, my husband, who put up with living in the 18th century for over a year.

Christina Richard
Tisbury, July 2018

AN INTRODUCTION

This book is the story of two men from a remote Wiltshire village, father and son Joseph and Josiah Lane, ordinary stonemasons , whose lives stretched across the Georgian period, from 1717 to 1833. They became grotto builders, men of artistic genius, acknowledged experts in their speciality, but the sort of ordinary craftsmen whose achievements are not normally recorded in the official pages of history, who deserve more recognition for their contribution to England's artistic history.

In the cult of the landscape garden grotto of the 18th century, these men were, each in his turn, the genius of the place. The mysterious, decorative, thrilling grottoes which appeared during that century in English gardens, were built to enhance the romantic landscapes created by rich landowners, in their attempts to delight visitors with a Virgilian experience, or to suggest being part of a painting by Claude Lorraine or Poussin. Yet many of these magical creations are the work of two poorly educated stonemasons from Tisbury, in south west Wiltshire, Joseph Lane and his son Josiah. From Stourhead to Fonthill, Wycombe Abbey, Wimborne St Giles, Bowood, Bowden Park, Painshill and Oatlands Park, Claremont, Castle Hill, Ascot Place, Belcombe and Norbiton House, Joseph and Josiah constructed brick, timber and limestone caverns, tunnels, bath houses , gambling dens and cascades. Some were profusely decorated with shells, coral spars, slivers of crystal, amethysts, feldspar and calcite fragments, some appeared savage and rough hewn. Venturing inside such a grotto the watery light from a lake or stream shimmered and refracted, thrilling the visitor as he took part in a knowledgeable voyage around his host's idea of classical antiquity and later, a more realistic or wilderness experience.

In order to bring Joseph and Josiah Lane and their family to life both in Tisbury and at the places where they worked, as much recorded, accurate information as possible has been used, taken from reputable published sources. These sources are biographies of their patrons, garden history by established, knowledgeable garden historians, and public sources such as the UK Parish Records, Census Returns, Wills and Probate Records , local history archives and Tithe Awards and their relevant maps. However, much of the written information has proved to be inconsistent, probably because new research is continually being undertaken and some information (for example where it can be found on the internet) is not necessarily in agreement with historical researchers. Or cannot be verified. In particular, written sources disagree about whether it was Joseph or Josiah who built and decorated which grotto (Josiah's name is better known), where they came from (Westbury and not Tisbury is occasionally mentioned), who died when and which William Beckford commissioned which grotto at Fonthill.

However, considerable effort has been made to ensure that the story of the lives of the Lanes works logically and chronologically. Speculation and imagination have played a part too , in imagining what life was like during that long Georgian period, and how it was experienced by both rich and poor.

So it is not all history, but neither is it a novel. The book aims to provide the reader with an idea of life in a Georgian rural village, the true story of a hard-working and comparatively successful working family, and how they lived, travelled and worked .

These two extraordinary men contributed so much to the elegance of England's wonderful 18th century gardens and although they are mentioned only fleetingly in recorded garden history, their story is worth telling. It was not only the rich, educated and much travelled aristocrats who created our landscape. It was the labourers, designers, craftsmen and gardeners who interpreted the wishes of their patrons, who also contributed.

Can the minimally known facts be set out and linked imaginatively to recreate believable and accurate life stories? Facts, known dates, deductions from these, more research, some assumptions and some, perhaps fanciful , ideas and then perhaps the life of the Lane family at home in Wiltshire and at work in the great English landscape gardens may emerge.

ILLUSTRATIONS

I

LIFE AT ASHLEY WOOD COTTAGE
GROWING AND LEARNING

In early 1717 Sarah Bowles realised she was pregnant. Sarah, the nineteen year old daughter of Mary and Henry Bowles had herself been born out of wedlock in Shaftesbury, Dorset and baptised there in January 1698.[1] Sarah was fortunate that her parents married later the same year, in September, thereby becoming a legally settled couple – under the hated Poor Law an unmarried mother could be bullied into naming the baby's father, or if he could not be found or would not help support his child, the mother might be forced to marry someone from another parish. This rather brutal treatment ensured that the mother's home parish did not have to take financial responsibility for the unfortunate mother and baby. The poor rate was levied against local citizens of each parish, the distribution of the meagre funds being dealt with by the local Overseer of the Poor, with final responsibility lying with the local Justice of the Peace.[2]

All this did not stop young girls from unwanted pregnancies, or even from getting pregnant a bit too early. Sarah, like her mother, was a lucky girl – the father of her baby, who would be named Joseph, did want to marry her. He was Thomas Lane, who lived at Ashley Wood Cottage and worked on the Fonthill Estate in Tisbury, in Wiltshire. Thomas may have come from Gillingham as the birth of a Thomas Lane is recorded in the Gillingham parish registers. That Thomas had been born in early 1680 and baptised in Gillingham in February of that year.

However a large Lane family had been resident in the Chilmark parish area (the next door village to Tisbury) for a long time, the first mention in the parish records being of John Lane, Husbandman, in January 1583. In a Pembroke Estate Survey of June 1631, there is a Thomas Lane living in a two roomed lofted-over dwellinghouse with the use of Voules Close, Barren Hill and The Close Above the Church.

Christopher Lane and William Lane both died in 1681 having made their Wills complete with Inventories of their possessions. They are classed as Yeoman, and William Lane's son Walter is definitely the grandfather of baby Joseph, as recorded in the Letters of Administration granted on Walter's death in 1748 to Joseph. There is no mention of Joseph's father Thomas, who must have predeceased his own father, but for whom there is no death record. Equally, there is no other Thomas Lane birth recorded locally. Perhaps his family were living in Gillingham temporarily.

Both Thomas and Sarah seem to have had stable family backgrounds. Sarah's mother Mary née Hillier, was born in the Hampshire village of Hurstbourne Tarrant, being baptised there in 1671. Her father, Henry Bowles came from one of the many Bowles families recorded around the Tisbury area at the time, some from Chilmark, Fovant or Teffont Evias. These are the main quarrying villages, so it is tempting to assume a tradition of quarrymen and stonemasons on the Bowles side of the Lane family. Indeed there is a Bowles Close marked on the later Tithe Map of Tisbury.

It also seems likely that Thomas Lane of Ashley Wood Cottage was a quarryman, stone cutter or stonemason. Ashley Wood is a small copse, now of mainly softwood trees, to the east of Fonthill Lake, which was not as wide then as it is today and had been formed by the first damming of the Fonthill Brook. Just below the wood and across a small field is one of the estate quarries - an easy distance to walk to work each day. Thomas' cottage and the estate of Fonthill in 1717 was owned by Francis, 1st Baron Cottington of Fonthill Gifford, a Roman Catholic peer. The main house on the estate at that time was known as Fonthill Antiquus. In a survey of the property prepared for Francis Cottington Esq. in 1660, an earlier member of the Cottington family, the house is shown as a substantial mansion with an elaborate gatehouse and a large, separate stable block. The house is pictured in 1700 facing east, with the

Fonthill Brook running through the walled front garden enclosures. At the rear of the property, according to the survey plan, is an elaborate knot garden, with yew hedges, avenues of trees and a large farmyard behind the stable block complete with central grain store raised on staddle stones. The cupolas of the entrance gatehouse are echoed by smaller entrance and exit gates from the gardens to the surrounding landscape.[3] On the hill to the south is depicted a mysterious dumbbell shaped enclosure, with a folly or viewing tower at its western end. The two circular ends are joined by a long grassed area. If this is in scale on the plan, and why would it not be – it is too long for a bowling green but perhaps the right length for an old tilting yard. It might have been used for hawking. No-one seems to be sure.

Fonthill already had a long history of habitation, as Fonthill Gifford had been acquired by Sir John Mervyn (1503-66) during the reign of Edward IV and passed down through his widow, his son, grand-daughter and then his grandson another Mervyn, 2nd Earl of Castlehaven. In 1631 the 2nd Earl was tried (by Lord Chief Justice Hyde, who happened to be the Earl's neighbour at Hatch House), for rape and sodomy, and was duly executed. Fonthill was forfeited to the Crown and subsequently acquired in 1632 by Francis Cottington Esq. After his death in Spain in 1652 the property passed down through his family and eventually to his great nephew's son Francis 1st Baron Cottington. There had been a brief ownership during the Commonwealth period by John and then Henry Bradshaw. John was a signatory to the death warrant of Charles 1, so his body had an unfortunate end – having been buried in Westminster Abbey with the usual pomp and ceremony, on the accession of Charles II his remains were exhumed, he was formally beheaded, and his body hung in chains for all to see. An early example of lessons will be learned.

Francis the 1st Baron no doubt hoped for a long and enjoyable life in his manor house at Fonthill, and although it is impossible to be sure, there must even then have been plenty of work on the estate for quarrymen and stonemasons, as although Fonthill Antiquus looks a solidly built mansion with its stable block, farm and estate buildings, all these would need repairs and improvements. Thomas Lane, living in his cottage at Ashley Wood, probably had plenty to do.

During 1717 Sarah came to live with Thomas and their baby was born sometime in the summer and baptised Joseph on 28 August that year. This is recorded as in Tisbury so his baptism would have taken place in the parish church of St John the Baptist, where the patronage

and incumbent clergyman was Thomas Marchant. It would have been
a long walk to the village centre from Ashley Wood, so perhaps Thomas
had access to a horse and cart (which he would have needed for work).
Joseph, although born out of wedlock, acquired 'settlement' in the parish
of Tisbury by being born there. His mother would only gain settlement
by marriage, so no doubt she was very happy later that year when
Thomas married her on 8 November, this ceremony being recorded as
at Fonthill Gifford, in the old church of St Nicholas. Curiously, Thomas
and Sarah had another marriage ceremony three days later, in Chilmark.
Perhaps this one was a more public event for their families and friends
and a chance for the baby to be admired. Thomas and Sarah had to
be married between eight o'clock in the morning and mid-day, by the
clergyman, before the communion table. The banns would have been
read three successive Sundays previously, this being cheaper than
buying a licence. Thomas and Sarah recited their vows and Thomas gave
Sarah a ring. Grains of wheat were traditionally scattered to encourage
fertility (although they had already proved their success at this by the
presence of baby Joseph) and the ceremony was followed by as much
eating, drinking and dancing as the family could afford.

Little Joseph survived his first six months, a great achievement.
Baby deaths were very frequent during the 18th C due to lack of hygiene,
malnutrition in both or either mother and baby, or simply because of
illnesses like diarrhoea, or typhus. Joseph would have been wrapped
tightly in a shirt, then a square of cloth from chest to feet, held in place
by a 3"strip of cloth – a 'roller', which was wrapped round and round
the baby. Finally a 'waistcoat' held his arms straight down his sides and
a shawl or blanket wrapped firmly around the whole bundle. His head
would be covered by one or more caps to protect it.[4] This system was
regarded as essential to help the body grow straight – it certainly kept
the baby quiet. At around four months his arms were freed from the
swaddling cloths and a few months later he was dressed in a simple
frock fastened at the back - the same garment being used for girls. Under
the frock Joseph wore trousers, a girl would have a petticoat. Padded
caps known as 'puddings' were used to protect toddlers' heads. When
Joseph was four he would be dressed in proper breeches and a jacket
over his shirt – sometimes the trousers and jacket were joined as one
loose garment by being buttoned together. As he grew older he would
wear linen drawers, breeches tied at the knees, a simple shirt under his
wool unlined jacket and an uncocked hat (i.e. not turned up at the sides).

His stockings were tucked under the edge of the breeches and his short lace-up leather boots were known as 'high-lows'.

Whilst he was still very small Sarah probably sang nursery rhymes to him and he would soon have learned the words and tunes of 'Jack and Jill', 'Old King Cole', 'Hey Diddle Diddle, the cat and the fiddle', 'Hickory Dickory Dock' and 'London Bridge is Falling Down'. Thomas probably made wooden toys for him – a rattle, a little cart, a wooden dog. He would learn to play ball, possibly to bowl a hoop although to do this a flat piece of road is needed and this was unlikely to be available around Ashley Wood Cottage.

Although Sarah was only nineteen when she had Joseph, there is no record of any brothers or sisters for him. This is unusual in that period; contraception was extremely difficult and many women were almost continuously pregnant, with the loss of children at all ages being an accepted, if no less tragic for the parents, fact. The records for Fonthill Gifford church are missing from between about 1720 to 1760, perhaps lost during the demolition of the old church and the building of the new one. There are two or three Lane marriages in the 1760s, Lydia to Thomas Harris in 1765, William to Sarah Hacker in 1768 and Hannah in 1770 to William Turner (Hacker and Turner are long established Tisbury families) but no baptisms which would confirm parentage, or burials which would fit in. It would be good to think that Joseph had siblings, but impossible to prove unless further parish records are eventually found.

Soon Joseph would be expected to help in the garden, learning to scare off the birds, dig, plant and water. Vegetables were a really important part of their diet and Sarah could grow beans, cabbages, onions, turnips and potatoes. Joseph picked up windfall apples, went blackberrying and collected eggs. The family had enough space around them in the clearing where the cottage stood, to let them keep a few hens, so occasionally an old hen could be casseroled as a main meal. They almost certainly kept a pig. On pig killing day there would be fresh liver, perhaps with dumplings, a great treat. The main pig joints would be salted and hung over the fireplace to mature as hams, or to be sold later when funds might be low. Belly pork was also preserved for bacon.

Bread could be bought or made at home. Tisbury's mill on the River Nadder had been in operation since 1086 and villagers and the smaller farmers brought their own wheat to be ground by the miller, or they bought flour from him.[5] Sarah would certainly have known how to make her own bread and this was essential as any shop was a long walk away.

It is unlikely that they ate much of the roast beef of Old England. Valued servants might occasionally receive a joint as a gift from the landlord, but as Cottington had a number of farm and estate labourers, it seems remote. If Sarah could buy a cheap cut of meat she could stew it slowly with vegetables and barley to make a nourishing, thick beef broth.

Although game was probably plentiful on the Fonthill Estate it would have been foolish for Thomas to take any. Poaching was a serious offence, even more so later in the century after the Game Acts were passed. This was a period when pheasants were first introduced and reared specifically for landowners to shoot. How tempting it must have been to put a few cider-soaked raisins under a tree to stupefy an unsuspecting bird. It wasn't worth it though, as poachers were shipped, or imprisoned for three to six months.[6] Snaring rabbits or hares was similarly punished.

No doubt Joseph went fishing – this could produce a nice fat trout for supper. He would have known the best pools in the Fonthill Brook, which ran from Fonthill Bishop down to Tisbury, where it was not overlooked. Like most little boys, he fished with a home-made rod baited with worms. There were almost certainly other estate children to go exploring and play with, or to go birds nesting in the nearby woods.

The family were lucky if they were able to keep a cow which could provide milk, the surplus being turned into cheese. The cow would have had to be turned out onto local common land and brought in to be milked. Most villagers, until the Enclosure Acts prevented this, relied upon the milk to vary and enrich their diets.

Everyone drank tea, rich and poor. It was expensive but it features as a separate and important item in all the income and expense accounts records of the period. It was essential to boil water for drinking anyway – although in the country some wells were perfectly safe. The East India Company reported 67,000lbs of tea imported in 1701 and a century later this had risen to 8 million lbs. The tea leaves were often mixed with other substances to reduce cost, and improve the company's profits, and servants from the big house would save the used tea leaves from the employers' tea table either for themselves or to sell to others.[7] Thomas and Sarah probably drank cider which was made locally, or they made their own. They would not have been able to afford imported wine, although they may have made elderberry wine and possibly beer. A family had to spend about two-thirds of its earned income on food and drink, leaving very little for rent, fuel, clothes and boots.

Life was regulated by sunrise and sunset. Workers got up early, breakfasted on bread and tea, went to work as soon as it was light, ate their dinner at noon and went back to work. If work was in the fields wives might bring bread, maybe cheese, and beer out to the field and work went on until dusk in winter, although in summer workers could go home, have supper and work in their gardens. Wives went on with the washing, trying to get clothes to dry, keeping the fire going, looking after the hens, the pig and the cow, cooking, preserving, pickling onions, making bread, mending and making clothes, cleaning the cottage and looking after the younger children.

On Sunday the family would, like every other family in the area, go to Church. Ashley Wood Cottage is quite a walk from the centre of Tisbury where the main parish church is. Perhaps the family worshipped at the old church of St Nicholas, Fonthill Gifford until 1747, when this church was demolished and the new Greek revival-style church of Holy Trinity was built, south west of Ashley Wood. There is a strong tradition of Dissension in the Tisbury area, with the first meetings being held in 1669 in the house of Samuel Coombes, in Chicksgrove. By 1725 there were numerous Dissenters, many of whom were quarrymen, although no Lanes are mentioned. There were enough Dissenting quarrymen and stonemasons to build their own Chapel, off the High Street in Tisbury. The quarrymen built this chapel at night with their wives and daughters guarding it against vandalism during the day.[8] Sadly it is said that the Anglican church encouraged this vandalism.

There was very little possibility of an education for young Joseph in the Tisbury area in the 1720s. A school was held in the village in the 1500s, but the last mention of it is in 1588. In 1740 the Alice Coombes Trust was set up so that the children of Tisbury could be taught to read, but by then Joseph was 23 years old and working.[9] He must have been a very bright young man, quick to understand and learn, as his subsequent work with grottoes had to be the result of interpreting and making a reality of ideas expressed by knowledgeable, well-educated architects, young men who had been on the Grand Tour, or ambitious landowners keen to impress their peers. Perhaps he was able to attend Sunday School, where he would have learnt his catechism and even how to read and write his name. It is more likely that he learned basic measurement and mathematical skills from his fellow workers and craftsmen and his father. He would grow up to be a strong young man, able to handle heavy weights, but with an artist's eye for textures, shapes and appropriate materials. He was ambitious, ready to take on whatever life offered. This proved to be exciting, giving Joseph the opportunity of some independence, travel within England and of meeting interesting artisans, craftsmen and even members of the aristocracy. How was he able to achieve this?

Joseph probably started work by helping his father on the Fonthill Estate. But by the time he was ten, he would be expected to earn money towards the family's living costs, and logically he would have been sent to work in one of the local working quarries. There is no record that he was officially apprenticed, but both the Lane and Bowles families came from Chilmark, where the great stone quarries were still in use, and the father of one of the quarry owners, William Privett, left an estate in Fonthill Gifford when he died. Family connections, or through his father meeting the older William Privett, could have made it possible for Joseph to start working in a substantial working quarry rather than the smaller estate quarry at Ashley Wood. Chilmark was within (rather long) walking distance of Ashley Wood. This is an assumption, but a realistic one as Joseph clearly learned his trade exceptionally well.

There were other quarries functioning in the immediate Tisbury area, but the stone was used only locally and not speculatively until John Moore & Co. acquired quarries in the mid 1750s.[10] Large quantities of stone for Fonthill Splendens were used from the Ashley Wood quarry, but again this was after 1750 – before that it would only have been quarried in a comparatively small way. Pyt House had a working quarry in 1725 and on the south side of Tuckingmill, Tisbury, there was a quarry known as World's End by 1769, with smaller quarries along Hindon Lane. Upper Chicksgrove was the earliest and largest quarry in Tisbury, being worked from the 1400s and is close to the great Chilmark and Teffont Evias quarries.

Most of Joseph's initial work as a boy would have been labouring. He needed to understand the use of windlasses, capstans, rollers and pulley wheels used to move the released blocks of stone, to grade and to sort and to load for transportation to the building site. He would learn how to measure, the use of geometry, economy of using the materials to avoid waste, to be safe in the quarry, and to understand and be able to identify the qualities of the stone needed for different jobs. He would attempt splitting, looking at the rift and grain, the axis of the stone, the use of wedges, possibly explosives, and all the various tools. Over the years he would become part of the stone-working brotherhood. It is a very ancient and honourable trade, highly skilled and, until the use of machinery, the way in which stone was worked did not alter for thousands of years. Strength and fitness were essential; an ability to work outside in all weathers and an artist's ability to recognise shape, volume, texture and suitability for the proposed building are all necessary skills. He would gradually acquire a collection of tools, and to learn to look after them. Tools for the stonecutter and mason can be used to fracture, cut, scoop, bash, shatter, tap gently, abrade and smooth. Each tool has its specific use and must be maintained in good working order. Each must be comfortable to the user's hand, in order to interact with the body, following the flow of the action created by intention and the use of muscles. Initially this can be a struggle or prove difficult in ensuring that the tool performs the required action, but with continuous use the tool becomes an extension of the mind and body. In stone cutting and masonry the knowledge of the type of material being worked, i.e. whether it is hard or soft, its consistency, brittle or flexible, its grain and crystalline structure are all intrinsic parts of the stonemason's skill. Balance and co-ordination play an important part, as the shift of energy occurs between the man, the tool and the stone. It is understandable that a master mason would wish to leave his own mark on a stone where he had been working.

Many years were to pass in learning, first as a trainee stonecutter, then as a stonemason, then as a master mason; this experience enabling him to understand create what an architect or client envisaged. A learnt process became intuitive and eventually, in Joseph's case, an art.

It is Autumn, in 1727. Joseph is out in the garden, digging. He is collecting worms so that he can go fishing. His father is nearby, lifting potatoes.

'Joseph' says Thomas and Joseph looks up from the crumbly brown soil, a pink worm dangling from his fingers. 'I met old Mr William Privett in the village yesterday evening. He says his son, who runs the big quarry at Chilmark, is looking for boys of your age to start learning the quarrying trade'. Joseph is ten years old. Father goes on 'You've been helping me with the estate repairs here at Fonthill for some time and your mother and I agree that it's time for you to be properly trained and to earn some money. We can't afford an apprenticeship but Mr Privett at Chilmark is a good man and will train

you well. This is a good opportunity. Your mother has taught you your letters and some numbers, so you should be able to understand what is expected of you'.

He looks affectionately at his son. It is quite normal for boys to start work at ten years old, but Thomas wishes that his son could go on enjoying his fishing, tree climbing and carefree life for a little longer.

Joseph drops his worm. He is quite shocked at the thought of having to go to work, although he knew it was going to happen soon. He's seen other boys from the estate start work, but he has been looking forward to his day's fishing with Will, the keeper's son. 'Do I have to go now?' he asks. 'No, no' his father laughs. 'We'll walk over to the main quarry on Saturday and meet Mr Privett. Mind you behave yourself and speak politely so that he takes you on' he adds. 'There will be a lot to learn and you'll need to listen and pick up information quickly and be willing to try any sort of work they ask you to do. You'll have to walk to work every day, so you'll need stout boots and some protective clothes'. Thomas says Joseph's mother will make him some new breeches and some bigger shirts.

Joseph is torn between pride that his father thinks he is ready for work, and anxiety that it will all be horribly frightening. What will it be like? He thinks he might enjoy meeting new people and finding out about other things, but his stomach feels a bit odd and his mouth has gone dry. It will all be so new.

Joseph picks up the worm which has been trying to wriggle back into the soil. He knows he has no choice, but today he will concentrate on fishing. He has something to tell Will, the keeper's son. He hopes there will still be fishing and trees to climb on his days off.

2

RURAL LIFE "IT WAS THE BEST OF TIMES, IT WAS THE WORST OF TIMES"

It was a time of elegance, a time of squalor; a time of mind-expanding travel and learning for the few and a time of restriction of movement, illiteracy and little education for the many. It was a time of plenty for some and poverty for most. A time when magnificent pillared and porticoed houses were built, while labourers lived in minimally thatched hovels with earth floors. A time of roast beef and claret for the rich but bread and small beer for the poor. A time when landowners would improve agricultural output by innovative ideas, methods and machinery while village labourers and small farmers saw their lives diminished and reduced as the common lands were enclosed by those landowners.

It was a time when power was still in the hands of the few, although discontent and dissent would spread insidiously through the poorer parts of society. While it became apparent that slavery was evil and should be abolished, few of the ruling class could admit that the majority of their own nation existed in some form of slavery too.

A time of extreme riches, luxury and indulgence, vast fortunes made from banking, from sugar, from trade or by inheritance contrasted with incomes which hardly covered rent and food and which often ended in illness, a pitiful sum of poor relief and eventually the workhouse. In short, it was Georgian England, between 1714 and 1834.

When Queen Anne died leaving no surviving children, her brother James as a Catholic, was barred from the throne and at the urging of the newly powerful Whig political party, a taciturn, distant German relative of the royal family, a man from Hanover, was proclaimed King. George I, as he became, immediately embraced the Whig party ideals and although the more Jacobite Tory party spent huge sums of money trying to regain control of Parliament, the Whigs remained in power between 1715 and 1760. The canny Hanoverian Georges understood that their entitlement to the throne depended upon the favour of Parliament. Royal power was gradually relinquished, leaving control in the hands of the 558 elected members of the House of Commons who were mostly wealthy landowners, and the House of Lords – 180 hereditary English or Welsh peers, 16 elected Scottish peers, and 26 Anglican Bishops. All were Protestants, Catholics being barred from office and from voting.

This powerful vehicle of State seemed very remote from rural Wiltshire, an extremely poor county at that time. Here the laws of the land were still administered by the King's appointed Judges, the local Justices of the Peace (mainly landowners), and the local manorial and ecclesiastical courts. More important to the Wiltshire villages were the churchwardens, the overseers of the poor and the constable. These local worthies ran the day to day parish business, from poor relief to pest control and the state of the highways. The manorial courts traditionally dealt with farm and cottage rents, tenancies, stray cattle, the problems of waste disposal, rules for the use of the common grazing land for tenants' sheep and cattle, and the rights to take stone, timber and fuel. These latter rights were eroded over the century when the commons were enclosed and by 1788 only a single court would be held and very few after 1800. Separate ecclesiastical courts oversaw the payment of tithes and other church related matters.[1]

Life could be very hard for villagers. It was essential to have work and never to become a burden to the parish. The ability to provide a decent life for the family was controlled in many ways, by an employer, the landlord, the parish and the church.

Opportunities to improve life were few – in order to move away from your native parish it was necessary to have found a job and a dwelling in the new parish, since the new parish was reluctant to take on any families unless they were seen to be self-sufficient, for fear of having to provide poor relief (the money for which was raised from local landowners).

The residents of the parish of Tisbury in the beautiful Vale of Wardour were perhaps luckier than many. Tisbury lies close to the great limestone quarries of Chilmark and had many smaller working quarries in the parish. Thus stone quarrying and dressing provided a valuable source of income both for the quarry owners and for the local quarrymen and stonemasons of whom there were many.

During the 18th century a number of large, elegant mansions were built in or close to Tisbury. The parish was already home to the Fonthill Estate, where the extended Fonthill Antiquus had burned down and the new owner, Alderman Beckford, built the magnificent Fonthill Splendens.

Pyt House at the other end of the parish was re-built in 1725 with a wonderful Ionic portico, and then was subsequently redesigned and altered by its architect owner John Benett later in the century.

Palladian New Wardour Castle designed by James Paine, the largest Georgian house in Wiltshire, was built between 1769 and 1776 for the recusant Arundell family, providing an elegant Roman Catholic chapel with an interior by Sir John Soane, and a Palladian mansion to replace the ruined old Wardour Castle.

These three houses provided work for stonemasons, carpenters, labourers, gardeners, plasterers, carriers and eventually of course, staff for the houses. And, of course, there was a continuous demand for dressed limestone from the local quarries.

Agriculture around Tisbury was dominated by the surrounding landscape; this is chalk country (cheese country being on the clay of northern Wiltshire). Sheep nibbled the grassland of the chalk downs and even richer grassland was provided by the water meadows of the Nadder Valley, which each year were covered by a flowing, thin sheet of water from the chalk streams and the river. This was cleverly diverted into channels and controlled by hatches, and run by the 'drowner', a workman of immense importance. This system provided an early feed for the sheep during the hungry months of Spring. To get that early grass, the water had to be kept moving and fresh, otherwise the grass rotted underneath it. Sheep were moved to higher arable land later, providing dung and urine as fertiliser.

Small farms and cottages provided food from gardens, and villagers were able to run a cow, a couple of pigs and a few sheep and chickens on the communal grazing lands, which were spread around the village, mostly in quite small blocks. This enabled families to survive with a reasonable variety of nourishing food, including milk and some cheese. After the Enclosure Acts during the latter part of the century, all brought in by local landowners consolidating and expanding their properties, this common land was taken away from the labouring classes, whose diet gradually became less and less varied, eventually resulting in malnutrition, illness and poverty. Agricultural practices improved, but the result could be near starvation for many.

At the start of the 18th century much of England had been cultivated for hundreds of years according to the 'common' system – there being three types of land – the arable fields, the common meadowlands and the commons or waste. Arable land was divided into strips, with many owners, some having only a few strips and some a considerable number. These strips were scattered among the arable fields, each strip being divided by either a furrow or a grass band, known as a fulk. However, the strips of all these different owners in a parish were cultivated on a uniform system agreed at the Manorial Court each year, and after the harvest, opened as pasture. The common meadowland was also divided and pegged out and after the hay harvest was taken, the meadows, too, became useful pasturage. The rough common or waste land was available as common pasture – it might be woodland, or roadside strips or a block of rough land. Until the Enclosure Acts, the Lord of the Manor had limited rights to the common or waste land - he had to allow enough common land for the needs of his tenants, although he retained mineral, surface and sporting rights for himself.[2]

A villager might be a freehold land owner, known as a yeoman. He might be a copyholder, lease holder or a tenant farmer, all of whom had different legal tenancy agreements, from short tenancies to leases that lasted for three lifetimes. In addition there were cottagers who owned their small properties, squatters who didn't, and farm or estate servants or workers living in employers' properties or in their employer's home.[3]

While villagers worked together in the fields, particularly at sowing, hay making and corn harvest; their cattle, pigs and sheep grazed together, their wives fetched home the family cow to be milked, or helped others with calving, lambing or farrowing; moved the sheep or helped to catch a goose at Christmas, this system encouraging a strong sense of community and social life. Maybe the cattle were in poor shape, any animal illness or infection spreading easily, production from the land a bit sparse in terms of the weight of corn per acre, but at least villagers could have bacon, the occasional joint of meat, the family cow produced milk, cheese could be made at home and vegetables could be grown in their own gardens. The small villagers' gardens provided a sense of independence – no-one could dictate what vegetables should be grown, there were no 'experts' telling cottagers how to grow, no magazine articles, no garden centres. Jane Brown in *The Pursuit of Paradise* comments on the bliss in the freedom of expression that revelled in healthy competition, a glut of beans or the pleasure of throwing a rotten egg over into the neighbour's patch.[4] Men who worked in the gardens of the great houses could bring home a small cutting of a favourite rose and what satisfaction must have ensued when it flowered all over the front porch. Plum, apple and damson trees provided fruit and many cottagers had hives for honey, which was valued as sugar was expensive. Their diet was reasonably varied and nourishing, even if there was no money left at the end of the week, or the debt got a bit bigger.

At the same time it was essential to have a trade. There were many occupations which provided needed services in the village – weavers, mill workers, shoemakers, tailors, butchers, bakers and candlestick makers, farriers, saddlers and blacksmiths, lacemakers, pedlars, charcoal burners, hurdle makers, carpenters and masons, barbers, household servants, gardeners, plumbers (who also did glazing) shopkeepers, mole-catchers, wet nurses and seasonal work for the bigger landowners.

There were other sources of income in Tisbury.

Although in the main cloth making in Wiltshire was in the north of the county, it seems likely that there were clothmakers in Tisbury – the names Tuckingmill and Weavelands certainly indicate this and it is recorded that two fullers were working in Tisbury in 1379. In the late 15th century a new fulling-mill was built, or maybe rebuilt, beside the Oddford Brook slightly to the west of the main village. References to four weavers in 1379, more in 1607 and a linen draper in 1616 and 1762 certainly imply that there was a cloth making trade.[5] In the 1820s a cloth factory was built at one end of Fonthill Lake, and this employed, for a short period, some 200 workers although some of these were reported as coming from Gloucestershire.

Tucking, or fulling, was the process by which cloth was cleaned, originally by the fuller 'walking' the cloth. He did this by standing in a barrel or trough of cold water containing a detergent – 'fullers' earth'. This labour intensive process became easier when water power was used to run a machine with two wooden hammers raised on tappets. The cloth was beaten by the hammers instead of the feet of the fuller. During the process the wool cloth shrank by about a third. Oil soap was in use as a detergent by the 18th century, and was used for finer cloths. After the cleaning, the cloth was stretched and dried on a tenter rack – a wooden frame erected near the fulling-mill, edged with blunt nails (tenterhooks) to which the edges of the cloth were attached evenly and tightly stretched. 'On tenterhooks', a phrase which entered the common language. Between 1727 and 1770 the finished cloth would be measured by inspectors, and 'sealed'. Fulling in Tisbury probably provided employment for a few men, and some women, who mainly did the stretching.

There was a tannery at the bottom of Duck Street, which made the whole area smell terrible, but created a few more employment opportunities. There were skinners and tanners from the 14th century and glovers in the late 1600s. One is reported as buying buckskins from Cranborne Chase and Grovely, so leather trades were another source of work.

Edge tools were made in the village, starting a tradition of agricultural tool and machinery making in the area and Thomas Osmond made watches and clocks. There were two malt-houses operating by the early 1800s.

The main source of additional income in the area after agriculture was quarrying. The local Portland stone quarries at Chilmark and Teffont Evias and the smaller ones in Tisbury provided many jobs and had been worked since before the Roman period. During the medieval years the stone was quarried for Wilton Abbey, the old and the new Salisbury Cathedral, parish churches, large country house, manor houses, local small houses and of course the village cottages. By the 18th century the quarries at Chilmark were in full production with two firms of stone cutters and stonemasons and were providing stone and workers for the building of Stourhead House, Longford Castle and Longleat House, together with stone for the fashionable follies and grottoes now considered essential for the gardens of the rich. Country women, in addition to running the household and the vegetable garden could make some extra money by knitting stockings, making straw bonnets and hats, lace making or elaborate button making. This all sounds like a busy and prosperous community, but many country workers at the beginning of the century lived mainly 'on the breadline'. This is illustrated by the record given by Roy Porter of an Oxfordshire rural labourer's expenses in keeping himself, his wife and their three children for one year:

4 ½ peck loaves a week at 1s 2d each	£13 13s
Tea and sugar	2 10s
Butter and lard	1 10s
Beer and milk	1 00s
Bacon and other meat	1 10s
Soap, candles etc	15s
House rent	3 00s
Coats	2 10s
Shoes and shirts	3 00s
Other clothes	2 00s
Total expenses	£31 08s

This man was a carter and digger, earning 8s. or 9s. per week, so his income was about £5 p.a. less than his expenses.[6] Poor relief, provided by the parish in the form of 'out relief' helped a bit but he was permanently in debt, with no means of making up this difference. No amount of cheerful socialising in the fields or in the pub afterwards would help in the long term – indeed a visit to the pub would have been a very infrequent pleasure. However, the view from some richer members of society was that those who worked irregularly were feckless[7]: As Dr George Fordyce commented:

> workmen are always idle when they have any money left, so that their life in spent between labour. . . . And perfect idleness and drunkenness.

At the same time taxation had become normal and was needed to service the ever increasing National Debt, which stood at £14.2 million in 1700, £130 million in 1763 and by 1800 had risen to £456 million. In 1700 the chief direct tax was the land tax, levied at 20%, but increasingly taxes became indirect, levied on consumption, and even on basic necessities so that in 1769 a foreigner commented that :

> the English are taxed in the morning for the soap that washes their hands; at 9 for the coffee, the tea and the sugar they use at breakfast; at noon for the starch that powders their hair; at dinner

for the salt that savours their meat; in the evening for the porter
that cheers their spirits; all day long for the light that enters their
windows, and at night for the candles that light them to bed[8]

Bricks, coal, leather and glass were also taxed. Not all of these
taxes might have affected a villager in Tisbury – how many people could
afford a wig – but certainly his basic needs were affected, soap, salt, tea
and sugar were essential. In fact, the common people of England paid
more in taxes during the 18th century than their French counterparts
before the Revolution. In addition corruption was absolutely normal
amongst the higher levels of society, with nepotism and back handers
accepted as normal practice. It is surprising that dissent, discontent and
desperation did not lead to successful revolt.

Housing for workers in the countryside varied across England,
from mud and thatch hovels to comparatively comfortable brick or stone
cottages. The stone cottages that constituted the main homes in Tisbury
are still scattered all along the lanes leading into the village's High
Street, where they cluster companionably around the medieval church
of St John the Baptist. Outlying farmhouses and their working buildings
are set firmly in the downland and little valleys surrounding the village
and the great estates of Wardour, Pyt House and Fonthill provide an
elegant framework of gardens, parks, lakes and woodlands. Tisbury has
never been invaded by a main road and is still the secret, beautiful and
hidden centre of the Vale of Wardour.

Cottages in the area, including those of the 18th century, were
fortunately stone built, mostly thatched and this abundance of stone
is due to the number of small working local quarries. Generally at this
period in Wiltshire and the South West, cottages tended to be poorly
built, having perhaps an earth floor and some even had earthen walls.
Few of these survive today. Most Tisbury cottages of the Georgian period
however, being built of stone, have survived the three centuries, and
some are even older. Generally, rooms when the cottages were erected
were small, with low front doors (people were smaller then). Sometimes
there is only one main room at ground floor level, although there might
be a partition providing a small, unheated extra room. The main living
was done in the larger space where there would be a stone chimney
breast, and all the cooking had to be done on a wood fire.[9] There might
be two small rooms above. Larger cottages had two or even three rooms
at ground floor level, a stone flagged floor, a bread oven extending

out from the chimney breast, the two smaller rooms being used as a parlour and a store-room or kitchen. Windows were provided with stone mullions to help with the weight of the stone and had a lip to throw off rain water.

The roof structure was of roughly cut oak, an A-frame resting on stone, with wooden laths covered in thatch. The chimney was generally at one end of the cottage, and if there was a bread oven, its semi-circular wall extending outwards would also be thatched. Beside the fireplace would be a narrow wooden staircase, although in more modest homes, the roof space could only be reached by a ladder. Party walls between terraced cottages had to be substantial, by law, to prevent fire spreading and any wooden eaves replaced by stone. Similarly wooden doors and any wooden window frames were to be recessed to reduce the risk of fire.

Life could be surprisingly cosy, if a bit cramped. Cottagers were able to collect starter sticks, furze and wood for the fire from the common land, and beds, however simple, could be warmed by a brick wrapped in flannel. Candles were expensive but people made their own lights from rushes dipped in fat, and stood them in metal holders.

There were no bathrooms, sanitation being very elementary, shared outside privies for villagers and a privy at the end of the garden for isolated cottages. No piped water either – water was pumped up from a well, or taken from a nearby brook. Much later Punch magazine published a parody of a poem by Felicia Dorothea Hemans, who idealized the cottages of the English countryside. The parody is nearer to the truth: The cottage homes of England, Alas! How strong they smell; There's fever in the cesspool And sewage in the well.' Nevertheless, the English were reputed to be very clean and according to Cesar de Saussure writing in 1720 -

> Though they are not slaves to cleanliness, like the Dutch, still they are remarkable for this virtue. Not a week passes by but well-kept houses are washed twice in seven days, and that from top to bottom; and even every morning most kitchens, staircase, and entrance are scrubbed. All furniture, and especially all kitchen utensils, are kept with the greatest cleanliness. Even the large hammers and the locks on the door are rubbed and shine brightly. English women and men are very clean; not a day passes by without their washing their hands, arms, faces, necks and throats in cold water, and that in winter as well as summer [10]

In spite of all this washing and cleanliness, and no-one can be sure it applied to the workers of Tisbury, the population of England fell in 1720 due to an increase in epidemics, typhoid fever causing many of these deaths, in 1718-1719, 1727-1731 and 1740-42.[11] This had the useful effect of increasing wages for artisans for a while, and during the same period a run of good harvests coupled with improvements in agricultural methods and management meant excess grain production. This did lead to lower bread prices, but then a surplus of grain was turned into spirits, particularly gin, which in its turn eventually caused more deaths. The cost of living dropped by 10% during the 1730s and 1740s but over production meant less income for farmers as corn sales prices dropped. Small farmers went out of business, releasing more land to larger landowners. Some areas were hit very hard, and in Warminster, not far away from Tisbury, conditions were reported as 'mud without and wretchedness within'.[12]

Tisbury, in spite of being in one of the poorest counties in England, nevertheless made progress during the first half of the 18c. It was home to a number of families, whose names have appeared in the parish Registers for three or four centuries, and still do. Some are easy to trace, appearing in those registers, on the gravestones in the churchyard, on the chapel walls, or the school rolls, or on the War Memorial plaques. This is the story of one family which came, lived here, gained some fame by virtue of hard work, and seems to have died out. It is unusual in that workmen's names tend not to be noted by historians, but the Lanes of Tisbury were different.

3

OPENINGS AND OPPORTUNITIES –
STOURHEAD

Meanwhile William Privett the Chilmark quarry owner had been providing stone for Henry Hoare (known as Henry the Magnificent) at Stourhead, where an expansive programme of garden buildings was underway, as Henry created his imaginative journey of the immortals, through heaven and the underworld.[1] William Privett and his stonemasons worked on the Temple of Flora in 1746, the Grotto in 1748, the Bridge in 1749 and the Pantheon (formerly the Temple) in 1755.[2] During this period Henry insisted on formal agreements with his contractors. For example, from the Ledger of Personal Accounts on the 6th September 1746 an Agreement was drawn up whereby – 'William Privett, Robert Moor the Elder and Robert Moor the Younger, Masons of the Parish of Chilmark in Wiltshire' contracted and were firmly bound to Henry Hoare of Stourhead' in the sum of £100 in an Agreement to erect and set up an Obelisk in the garden of Stourhead; the stone to be brought from their Chilmark quarries. Henry bound them in the sum of £100 which would guarantee 'the stone to be flawless, to be sound and good against any weather for five years from finishing and completion of the Obelisk, which was to be built in a workmanlike manner'. William

Privett signed this Agreement in the presence of Joshua Cox and Roger Helleker.[3] William's workers made good his promise and work on the Obelisk went ahead, the eventual billing coming to a price of £349 17s.4d. Presumably William and the two Robert Moors did not suffer the loss of the £100 guarantee.

If the assumption that Joseph Lane trained by working for William Privett at Chilmark is correct, then Stourhead is the start of his career in grotto making. Not only is it likely that Joseph was known to the Privett family, through work at the quarry, another connection is possible in that William Privett's father, another William, who died in 1747, in his Will left a small estate at Fonthill Gifford, so it is certainly possible that the Lane family was known by the Privetts.[4] Communities were smaller and people with a common interest very likely to be known to one another.

By the time William Privett was commissioned to build at Stourhead in about 1744, Joseph, now aged 27, must have become an experienced stonemason, having worked at Fonthill and Chilmark quarries and possibly Alderman Beckford's new buildings. The Alderman, a colleague of Henry Hoare's, banked with Hoare & Co. and so knew him socially too. What could be more natural then, for the Alderman when talking to his neighbour about their respective garden improvements, to recommend the young stonemason? Of course this is yet more speculation, but another realistic possibility.

And so to work on his first grotto. The workmen presumably travelled on the carts with the stone, and would have had to lodge in estate buildings, of which Stourhead had a number, including the stable courtyard. First the stone had to be cut and loaded onto the carts. The carter was an important part of the work, and there is a bill in the Stourhead accounts for a Mr Mereweather as one of the carters for the grotto stone. From Chilmark, the carts, laden with stone, would join the road coming from Wilton, which passed through Fonthill Bishop at the northern end of the park. No doubt Joseph could have joined a cart at the Fonthill road junction, travelling on to Hindon, where after a couple of miles, the road turned right to join the Shaftesbury to Warminster road. The hills were steep after this, and the track had to wind its way west and up to join the old Harroway which eventually passed close to Stourhead where Alfred's Tower now stands. The carts could then drop down into Stourhead to unload in the working area which was to become the garden. The workers were expected to be available for quite long periods, probably not getting home to Chilmark and Tisbury very often.

However, before Joseph could become involved in working on the Grotto, Henry Flitcroft, architect and designer for the garden buildings at Stourhead, wrote in a letter dated 25th August 1744[5] to Henry Hoare concerning 'a Temple of Ceres, with the Rocky Arch on which I propose to place the River God, and a sketch of how I conceive the head of the lake should be formed. Twill make a most agreeable scene'.

The River God figure to which he refers was a lead sculpture by Thomas Manning bought by Henry Hoare in 1743. It no longer exists at Stourhead and its fate is unknown. The Temple of Ceres (subsequently Flora) was built overlooking a stretch of water formerly the estate stew pond (a pond used for storing fish). Below Flitcroft's classical, pedimented temple sits a rocky arch, with a recess into the bank. This is all that now remains of the feature designed by Flitcroft. Originally it had a pediment, and inside the rocky arch reclined the River God. Below him a cascade fed by the natural spring in the bank tumbled down over tiered steps to the canal. Whilst the pediment was of dressed stone, the rockwork exterior was built of the tufa-like stone said to have come from

Stourhead, Wiltshire: The Pantheon, the Hermitage and the grotto from the lake

Italy but similar to that used by Joseph later at Painshill and which came from quarries in the Bath area. The feature was constructed on brick foundations on timber pilings.[6] This feature pre-dates the main Grotto, as at the time the canal had not yet been linked to the other ponds to form the Great Lake.

In 1748 the central part of the main Grotto was built. This is on the southern side of what became the Great Lake, facing the Stone Bridge across the water. At the time the Grotto was first built, by Mr Privett's stonemasons, the water level was much lower, possibly by up to 1 to 1.5 metres lower, and the spring which feeds the water feature inside the Grotto chamber comes from a source considerably higher up the bank, thus allowing the water to enter the Grotto, flow down into the cold bath, then being channelled out under the pebbled floor, into what became the Great Lake. At the present time, the water having risen, the floor of the Grotto is level with the lake, but when the central chamber of the Grotto was built, the spring water exited the Grotto through a hole under its lakeside arch and down over shallow, wide steps before losing itself in what was withy beds and a deep pool. This must have made walking around the front of the Grotto rather slippery, although it

Stourhead: the grotto

may have looked elegant, and added to the watery sounds. Perhaps the intention always was to join up the various ponds and the stew pond/ canal and a rise in the water was anticipated. There is still a considerable flow of spring water through the Grotto and out into the lake.

As Mr Privett's stonemasons are recorded as having worked on Flitcroft's Temple of Flora, it seems sensible to suggest that they are also responsible for the work on his Rocky Arch and then on the Grotto itself. The Nautical Archaeological Society attributes the design of the Grotto to Henry Flitcroft,[7] but it seems impossible to be absolutely certain. Flitcroft is recorded as responsible for the design of the other Stourhead buildings, such as the Temple of Apollo, the Temple of Flora, the Obelisk, the Druid's cell, Alfred's Tower and the Pantheon. Taking into account the significance of the position of the Grotto on the circuit, and its importance in the story from the scenes of Aeneid, it seems very likely that it too would have been designed by him at Henry Hoare's request, at the same time, as an important part of the classical circuit experience. Naomi Miller in her 1982 book Heavenly Caves, attributes the grotto to Henry Flitcroft - she includes it in the list of buildings Henry Flitcroft designed for Stourhead. And suggests that Joseph Lane 'may have had a hand in building the Grotto at Stourhead'. Mr Privett himself is sometimes given the credit for building the grotto, but the actual work would probably have been by his employees, the stonemasons from Chilmark.

However, the Grotto in 1748 was not the same as it is now. The main, central chamber was built in 1748, the spring being diverted into a clay tank behind it, to emerge in a controlled manner into the cold water bath in the central chamber. The Swedish architect F M Piper later (1779) drew detailed plans and a cross section for the Grotto, showing the route the water takes to reach the Great Lake, but his cross section fails to show the shallow steps which have been found by the archaeologists, in front of the Grotto mouth. These drawings, made in 1779, show that the central Grotto, which is of fairly regular stone construction, has sprouted side chambers clearly built in a more natural, rocky looking style, consistent with later garden fashion. It has a not quite twisting entrance tunnel, and exit steps. It faces the lake, with its entrance almost at water level as you travel around the designed walk. Facing the Grotto from the lake, at the right hand side is the narrow, dark tunnel entrance, hidden by shrubbery and trees. Once you have plunged into its dark depths, the tunnel opens into a patterned pebble floored chamber, and then through a dark archway into the central room where a nymph lies sleeping on a black marble plinth, while water splashes down around her into an overflowing shallow pool and then out into the lake, which can be seen opposite her, framed by an uneven rocky surround. Below her are lines translated by Alexander Pope from a Latin verse by Cardinal Bembo - 'Nymph of the grot, these sacred springs I keep . . .

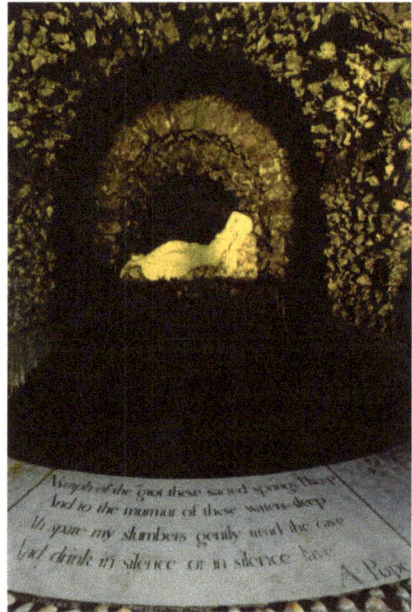

Stourhead: the Nymph of the Grot (left), and the River God (right) by John Cheere

The chambers in the grotto at Stourhead are simply decorated, lined in flint, pebbles and tufa from Italy. There are niches for candles, and small alcoves to sit in and contemplate the view to the lake. The central chamber is illuminated by the light reflecting off the water of the lake, where the bridge and glimpses of the rest of the garden can be seen. Continuing through another narrow space you enter the cave of the River God. The statue, which once held a trident, is seated on an Italianate tilted jar, from whence flows the source of the River Stour. An exit up fern-fringed steps was added later. In the early years the exit would have been to go back from the River God's cavern through the central chamber and to creep out again under the rustic pediment. Both the nymph of the grot and the River God were sculpted by John Cheere in around 1751.

Apparently the jagged arch with its view to the river had, in 1765, a 'sort of Curtain, when you chuse it' according to Joseph Spence so that bathers in the pool could be protected from prying eyes looking in from the lake. Henry Hoare would bathe here naked, with friends, all to the sound of two French horns playing in the acoustically perfect chamber of the grotto. As he says 'a Souse into that delicious Bath and Grot, fill'd with fresh Magic, is Asiatick Luxury and too much for Mortals'.[8] Presumably a rich banker is more than Mortal.

In 1748 William Privett delivered his bill to Henry the Magnificent for the stone and the work done at Stourhead for the grotto.[9] It specifies

William Privett's invoice for the stone and work on the Stourhead grotto 1748

the various types and cuts of the stone delivered, the cost of the hours of workmanship both at his quarries (37 working days) and at Stourhead (935 working days) and his own daily fees for 101 days' work. This came to £186 5s. 2d.[10]

The entrance and exit passages and the exit steps were added later, the passages probably in 1765, and the steps in 1776. Could Joseph have had a hand again in 1765? The style of the passages would indicate his involvement. In 1764 he had finished the preliminary work at Painshill, using the tufa-like Bath stone for the exterior of the Painshill grotto. He went home to Tisbury but it was not until 1766 that he started work at Castle Hill in Dorset, so there is a gap in working time which might well have been filled by a return to Stourhead for Mr Privett, to add the passageways. By this time Josiah too might have joined him, being 13 years old and useful to his father. In 1775 however, he started the work at Oatlands Park, and this went on for some years, so it is extremely unlikely he had a hand in the final work to the grotto, the steps leading up and back to the circuit.

In 1780 Horace Walpole, the 4th Earl of Orford is minded to make a comment about the Grotto. Walpole was an almost exact contemporary of Joseph Lane having been born on 24th September 1717 (Joseph in August 1717) and dying a few years after Joseph, in 1797. Walpole however, was a very well educated aristocrat, a writer, connoisseur of fine arts and antiques, builder of the idiosyncratic Strawberry Hill Gothick House and a politician of the Whig persuasion. He felt himself very well qualified to comment on the fashions and achievements of his contemporaries, sometimes wittily, but often in a cutting or sarcastic fashion. In the case of Stourhead, he writes approvingly:

> Grottoes in this climate are recesses only to be looked at transiently. When they are regularly composed within of symmetry and architecture, as in Italy, they are only splendid improprieties. The most judiciously, indeed most fortunately placed grotto is that at Stourhead, where the river bursts from the urn of the god, and passes on its course through the cave'

This grotto is the template for all the subsequent grottoes built by Joseph and his son. No doubt Joseph learned from his experience here all about the idea of the grotto and its place in the garden. He seems to have been able to assimilate ideas quickly and to interpret, improve and embellish the designs that his patrons requested. Joseph was good at making the most of the opportunities which were offered to him and not being worried about travelling considerable distances, probably in discomfort and being away from his family for long periods. Sometimes this must have been hard for his young wife Deborah, as we shall see.

Meeting Mr Flitcroft

Joseph is enjoying himself. It is a cold day but the sun is out and the water in Mr Hoare's new lake is shimmering. He has been working on the Temple of Flora, carefully assembling the beautifully cut stones that Mr Mereweather the carter delivers from Chilmark. Below him stonemasons are working on the Rocky Arch and its cascade. Today he can see the gardeners digging holes for the young trees that have just arrived from the tree nursery. They are small, but Joseph knows that they will grow quickly and the great garden around him which he thinks looks at present like a battlefield, will settle down, the grass will grow and the limbs of these young saplings will shape the landscape. He doesn't know how Mr Hoare decides where to plant them, or how the colours will change during the year, but he knows enough from the Fonthill landscape to appreciate what Mr Hoare is doing on this great site.

Mr Privett arrives on a cart full of cut stones. 'Joseph' he says,' come with me'. Joseph clambers up on to the cart which jolts slowly round the edge of the water, towards the ponds on the far side. A gentleman dressed in breeches and a green frock coat, his wig nearly hidden under his cocked hat, is standing by the water's edge, carrying a large roll of paper under his arm. He is looking at the bank of earth and stones beside the lake. Joseph's gaffer, Mr Privett, gets down from the cart and Joseph follows, to stand near the horses and politely to one side.

'Good morning Sir' says Mr Privett. 'Mr Henry Flitcroft?'

'Indeed Sir' says the elegant gentleman, tipping his cocked hat in return. 'And is this the young man who is to help with the Grotto?'

'It is, Sir. His name is Joseph. Joseph Lane of Tisbury. He turns to Joseph. 'Joseph, you will be working here now for Mr Flitcroft, who has designed A GROTTO' He will explain it to you and I will be arranging for the stones and other materials he requires to be delivered to the site when necessary'.

And off goes Mr Privett as briskly as the horses and laden cart will allow. He is a busy man, with the responsibility of producing the stone for whatever it is that Mr Hoare has next dreamed up for his garden. The carter winks at Joseph before he leaves and Joseph is comforted. They will drop the dressed stones off elsewhere in the garden and Mr Privett will return to Chilmark to supervise the cutting of the stones for the next stage of the garden buildings.

Joseph and Mr Henry Flitcroft look at one another. Mr Flitcroft is an architect and gentleman and Joseph Lane a worker. They know their places but somehow they know that they will be able to work together. Mr Flitcroft takes Joseph by the arm and they sit down. Together they unroll the unwieldy sheet of paper which is covered in straight and curved lines and notes. They weight it down with stones on each corner. It is incomprehensible and Joseph swallows. He has to admit he doesn't understand it at all.

'Can you explain this to me?' he asks, shyly.

Henry likes the look of this young man. He reminds Henry of his younger self. After all, he himself was the son of a gardener, and fortunate to have been trained as an architect. 'Of course' he says and starts to talk. They look at the plan, turn it around and look at the site, imagining how the drawing will translate into stones and mortar, marble and flints. Henry tells Joseph there will be a team of labourers working on THE GROTTO and he hopes that Joseph will help to organise them. Joseph begins to see how this will work – the narrow entrance, the discovery of the interior rooms, the glimpses of the lake and the bridge, how to channel the source of the river tour into the rooms and return it to the lake, (how?) and he imagines the snow white Nymph (what exactly is a Nymph?) and the great River God which Henry tells him are being sculpted by the well-known Mr Cheere. Well known to Henry maybe, but all new to Joseph. Mr Cheere, the Nymph and the River God – all alien beings – what will it all look like and why does Mr Hoare want such a thing in his garden?

Henry goes over the plan again and decisions are made about where to start work tomorrow. The team of labourers will arrive and Joseph needs to be able to use them straight away. Practical matters are discussed. After this Henry goes on to explain how THE GROTTO will be part of a thrilling walk for Mr Hoare's guests, around the lake and the gardens. THE GROTTO must be a dark mysterious place, where imagination can be let loose. Will it be frightening when you enter, or will it be a place of beauty, revealing the spirit of the garden? The genius of the place. Joseph likes that phrase. It will be his task to interpret Mr Hoare's vision of a descent into the underworld, the discovery of the gods living there, the rebirth of hope and an escape into the sublime surroundings above. Henry refers to the genius loci – and Joseph listens with interest to these mysteries, although he thinks it all a bit far fetched. Nevertheless he is keen to understand and to learn from Henry, so he keeps quiet and allows his head to be filled with ideas and possibilities.

4

GRAND TOURS AND GREAT GROTTOES

By the mid 18th century it was almost a traditional rite of passage for a rich young man to undertake the 'Grand Tour'. To become socially acceptable in Georgian society one simply had to travel through Europe, acquiring en route an awareness of differing cultures, an ability to converse in French and Italian, make social and business contacts abroad and learn to dress and behave stylishly.

It was all very well to have learnt Latin and Greek at school, but culture in England was limited at that time; there were few paintings to see other than one's family portraits, no galleries, artistocratic houses were still medieval or only slightly improved and gardens very formal. It would be exciting to be travelling, even if with one's tutor or guardian (known as a 'bear-leader'). A couple of valets, a musician and a painter and some servants would make up the party. The 'bear leader' was there to look after the young man, get him out of any scrapes, encourage his education and manage his financial affairs. The image is of a simple minded bear being led about on a string, after a painting by James

Hay.[1] Most of these young men had little idea what to expect. Travelling could be dangerous, the roads in Europe were known to be much worse than the newly created turnpikes of England. There were bandits (take a pistol with you) and the inns were indescribably disgusting. Foreign doctors were well known to be all quacks, so it was essential to take a proper medicine chest. Passports and money had to be arranged – money being in the form of letters of credit from one's English bank could be carried safely and would be honoured on presentation in an equivalent European bank.

First the unsettling Channel crossing in a heaving packet boat for up to 36 hours which caused much seasickness. Having arrived on foreign shores, a carriage would be hired and then where? Paris, of course, to acquire new clothes, wigs, boots and scent. Perhaps a visit to the dancing master with lessons in deportment. Acquiring social graces would also include lessons in love and how to manage an affair elegantly. After these exertions a gentle visit to the Galeries du Louvre would be in order, and for those who were suitably connected, an introduction at the Court of Versailles, to wonder at the great gallery of mirrors and at the Royal family.

On to Italy, but there were obstacles in the way – the enormous mountains of the Alps - the chilly, intimidating vastness of the mountains compared with the Lake District or even the Scottish Highlands. To cross those mountains over the Mont Cenis pass route entailed leaving the carriage (which would be dismantled and loaded onto mules for the pass) and transferring to an 'Alp-machine', which was in fact a sedan chair attached to two poles, carried by four porters.[2] On alighting from the Alp machine, the traveller boarded a sled for the terrifying descent down to the mountain into Italy, where he rejoined his reassembled carriage and new horses.

Having achieved the crossing of the Alps it was on to Venice. Culture, exorbitant costs, and courtesans were now the order of the day. The latter often resulted in something quite nasty, requiring rest and recuperation. No doubt the great altar and wall paintings in the numerous Venetian churches were a little compensation for the suffering. These must have been considered amazing, since wall paintings in English churches had been piously whitewashed over by the pleasure loathing Puritans in the previous century. Venice had an overload of gold and ornamentation, colour and glass, glittering (if dirty) canals and peach coloured palaces. Intrigue abounded, masked balls hid identity and

Venice thrived on decadence and tourists. How better to spend the morning admiring the basilica of St Mark and then sitting at Florian's in the piazza for a morning hot chocolate. An afternoon's siesta with a young lady and then a meeting with – well who knew what might happen? No doubt the bear leaders had to keep an eye on the innocent bears.

And on to Florence, which was more cultured, more elegant and more refined in every way. Pictures to view, private palaces to see and Sir Horace Mann (the British representative in Florence for some fifty years) to meet in the Tribuna at the Uffizi Palace, the centre for the visiting Grand Tourist, where everyone met up to take tea and discuss the merits of the statues, paintings and objets d'art. One was becoming quite educated by now and Rome would add a further layer of sophistication.

All roads did eventually lead there and it would be the ultimate enlightenment moment. Visiting the ancient classical ruins and sculptures, the Colosseum, the Pantheon and the experience of being in the very places they had learned about during all those tedious Latin lessons, was thrilling. The guidebooks suggested three hours of sightseeing each morning, but one could take one's time, relax and not work too hard at all this culture. The countryside around Rome, the Appian Way, the villas and the temples all needed to be appreciated and then there were the gardens, Virgil's Arcadia, the Tivoli and the Villa d'Este. One could also spend delightful hours bargaining for artefacts and paintings. Many Grand Tourists took home carriages full of paintings, sculptures, Etruscan vases and even classical columns which found their way into the redesigned, classically embellished English landscape.

Some fortunate Grand Tourists planned to be present in Rome in late June to see the fireworks which celebrated the festival of St Peter and St Paul. Others might have been able to view the celebrations which followed the election of a new Pope.

The last stop on the Grand Tour was generally Naples and its surrounding marvels; Vesuvius, the Elysian fields, the newly discovered Herculaneum and Pompeii. If one was rich it was possible to finance a new archaeological excavation and thus carry off freshly found artefacts.[13] Naples was certainly not very hygienic, giving rise to the phrase 'see Naples and die', but one was becoming used to managing in unpleasant inns and although some unfortunate people, including some servants, a musician or two, and the odd valet, succumbed to diseases, most young gentlemen survived to tell the story of their journey.

And then the French revolted, Britain went to war with Napoleonic France and the great Grand Tour came to an end. A few unlucky British were trapped in France and interned for some years. The Grand Tour however had a significant effect upon the British landscape, creating great art collections and particularly the new architecture based on the classical ideas expounded and demonstrated in and around Venice by Andrea Palladio. Amongst these great shifts in style was to be the fashion for a Virgilian landscape to surround the new classical mansion, and in the landscape would be a lake, a temple or two, perhaps a ruined archway and a mysterious grotto.

But what is a grotto and why did it become so desirable for an 18th century gentleman to have one in his landscape? The word comes from the Greek krupta – vault, and the Latin crypto – both mean hidden or concealed, and the English meaning has come to include both a natural or artificially hidden place, sometimes decorated, sometimes rougher or more rugged. The Latin crypto is also tied to cryptoportico, a subterranean corridor, or linking passage between villas or buildings,[4] such as the Grotto of Seiano near Posillipo, Naples, where a tunnel consisting of a series of brick arches with tufa walls, some 700 metres in length provides a dramatic entrance to the Vedor Polliana villa at Pausilypo and its complex which includes an Odeion (a roofed theatre), a Temple, a Sacrarium, a Nymphaeum and a 2,000 seat amphitheatre.

Entrance to Font de Gaume SW France

West Kennet Long Barrow Wiltshire

Caves, vaults, and underground passages have for thousands of years been associated with places of sanctuary, spirituality, rites of birth and death and both feelings of terror and of safety. Hence the many sites, particularly around the Mediterranean, which are either underground, or built to imitate being underground, which have a special significance for humans. Very often the source of a spring, natural caves were revered as sacred places, places of healing and of contemplation. The caves of South Western France at Font de Gaume and Lascaux, with their symbolic paintings are very early examples now thought to have been used as shrines 14,000 years ago; as are the stone chambered Neolithic long barrows of Wessex, where the dead were buried accompanied by sacred rites. The Greek 4th century BC Plutonium – a grotto at Eleusis – is connected with the cult of Demeter and her search underground for her daughter Persephone. Some were consecrated to the God Pan, or to Apollo or to the nymph of the spring, but many were simply a place of safety or a natural wonder as are the stalagmite and stalactite caverns of the Peloponese and Crete.[5] In the Roman period Emperors created decorated grottoes for their villas, as at Hadrian's remarkable Tivoli villa. The Emperor Tiberius, who moved to Capri in 27AD, bathed in the sea caves of the Island, particularly the one known as the Blue Grotto, with its narrow, low entrance from the sea. He decorated the inside of the Blue Grotto with statues of Neptune and Triton, who according to Pliny the Elder, was 'playing with a shell', Other sea caves such as the coral cave, are naturally decorated with corals, stalactites and lit by shafts of sunlight entering through narrow apertures creating brilliant colour changes, emerald greens, brilliant turquoise and intense blues.

Nor can we ignore the sanctuaries mentioned in the Old Testament, or the tombs and temples of Jordan's ancient city of Petra. In Jerusalem original masonic symbols survive in the underground quarries which provided the stone for Solomon's temple, and where the stonemasons had their secret meeting places. Early Christian biblical references mention the Grotto of the Nativity, the Grotto of the Garden of Gethsemane and under the great Basilica of the Holy Sepulchre, the Grotto of Calvary was embellished by the Emperor Constantine with 'selected columns of abundant ornamentation' so that the grotto 'shone under a glittering adornment. These Christian symbols of life and death then appear in late Medieval and Renaissance paintings – as caves in the detailed landscape backgrounds, as a grotto in Leonardo's Madonna of the Rocks and in the tiny background landscapes of the Northern Renaissance painters who undertook travel to Italy or pilgrimages to the Holy Land.

It is hardly surprising then, that Renaissance architects and builders, looking back at a classical antiquity for inspiration, created their own versions of the sacred Grotto. A man-made structure could be camouflaged to appear as a natural feature in the landscape, or a classical temple could, on entrance by the visitor, reveal a highly decorated, atmospheric, stony, mossy watery cavern. This could be beautiful, or occasionally grotesque, as at the Sacra Bocco (Gate of Hell) built in the Bormarzo Gardens between 1500-1570 for Pier Francesco Orsini. This gaping-mouthed cavern, with its teeth, staring eyes and terrifying entrance was surely inspired by Dante's words 'All hope abandon ye who enter here'. What terrors might be awaiting the unwary visitor? In fact the frightening black hole leads to a simple chapel-like interior with a white stone bench and table.

Another prime example of the Renaissance style is the Grotto Grande in the Boboli Gardens of Florence in Italy, built in the late 1500s for Duke Francesco 1 de Medici, partly by Vasari and finished later by Buontalenti. Although this grotto has the requisite stalactites, a water feature and statuary inside it, the façade is the classical order, in stone blocks, with a courtyard entrance. Not terrifying at all. Many of the Renaissance grottoes combined water features with decorations of shells and coral, some featuring designs of birds, animals or masks, a fantastical interior experience set in a formal classical building.

In France grottoes tended to the theatrical, with mechanical jokes played upon the visitor, such as automata squirting water upon the unwary. A Huguenot grotto maker and ceramic artist by the name of Bernard Palissy designed a cave in the form of a coiled shell, with an enamelled interior, the cave to be covered entirely with earth and trees. This was to be a place of retreat and meditation, but Palissy's designs were seldom completed.[6]

Posillipo, Naples by Pitloo 1826

These continental grottoes, visited by the young English gentlemen on their Grand Tours, were, together with the ruins of the original Roman and Greek temples and pavilions, the inspiration for the sudden enthusiasm for the classical landscapes created by them on their return to England.

By the time the English had taken up these ideas, nearly a hundred years after the Renaissance, the grotto had become theatrical scenery, the proscenium arch opening onto a scene of illusion. The new style used hydraulics to create water fantasies, with shell decorated walls and mythical figures of sea monsters, satyrs and gods which might suddenly spout water. Another Huguenot, Salomon de Caus, worked in Europe in the late 1500s on this style of grotto and his younger brother Isaac continued the ideas, producing the gardens and grotto at Wilton House near Salisbury in Wiltshire between 1649 and 1653. This was in the classical style, with Triton blowing a conch shell, and Venus riding with Cupid on a shell across the water.[7] The sound of birds singing was created by the movement of water and air. This grotto was considered to be the finest in the land. At Woburn Abbey the shell patterned grotto is inside the great house and the visitor has to ascend rather than descend into it. It was a cool place, the opened loggia facing north and was said to be a healthy place to be, which was essential, as the Duke of Bedford had it built during the years he lived at Woburn trying to escape the plague ridden streets of London. This room is grotto as art, as decoration, but not as nature – the theme is watery and Horace Walpole called it the 'Bathing Room'.

Alexander Pope was a grotto enthusiast and had written on the great gardens at Stowe:

> To swell the Terras, or to sink the Grot;
> In all, let Nature never be forgot. . . .
> Consult the Genius of the Place in all,
> That tells the waters or to rise, or fall. . .

But when he built his own tunnel and grotto in 1725, it had to be much more art than nature, as he did not have the landscape, the space, or the choice of where to put it. In order to reach his Thames-side garden from the front garden of his house at Twickenham, he had to excavate a tunnel under the Hampton Court road. Brilliantly, he devised rooms leading off the rocky tunnel and decorated them so cleverly with pieces

Alexander Pope in his Grotto at Twickenham by William Kent

of mirror, shells and minerals that the mirror managed by reflections and angles to appear as if there was moving water within the grotto, the shifting greys and greens of the Thames, or flashing blue in summer.[8] Pope, as a well-educated poet, understood the metaphysical associations of caves. He was a Roman Catholic in an Anglican society, and his grotto became a place of contemplation, safety and withdrawal from life, whilst still being a place of beauty to share with his many friends. Even Horace Walpole admired it, writing;

> The passing through the gloom from the grotto to opening day; the retiring and again assembling shades; the dusky groves, the larger lawn . . . disposing Plates of Looking glass in the obscure Parts of the Roof and Sides of the Cave

And a contemporary description in the Newcastle General Magazine;

> Cast your Eyes upward and you half shudder to see Cataracts of
> Water precipitating over your Head, from impending Stones and
> Rocks while salient Spouts rise in rapid Streams at your Feet

Alexander Pope continued to enjoy his grotto, making alterations
to it as his interest in geology expanded. He collected minerals from
Cornwall, layering them out in their original strata so that his visitors
could; 'Approach, Great Nature studiously behold'.

Pope's influence on the English grotto cannot be overstated, and
so it is appropriate that at Stourhead, where nature begins to be equalled
with art, his are the words that the visitor remembers[9]:

> Nymph of the grot, these sacred springs I keep,
> And to the murmur of these waters sleep;
> Ah, spare my slumbers, gently tread the cave.
> And drink in silence, or in silence lave!

And so, following Pope, the grotto becomes one of the most
desirable, almost essential elements of the picturesque English 18th
century garden.

5

PATRONAGE AND PROGRESS

At Fonthill a change was taking place. In 1745 the estate, comprising the house, the church, the village and 3,000 acres was sold to William Beckford, known later on as Alderman Beckford. The Alderman had been born in Jamaica where his family owned a number of sugar plantations and a great many slaves. He had been sent to Westminster school in 1719 where he made friends who would be influential in his future life, going on to Balliol College Oxford to study medicine. He obtained his BA degree in 1729 at Balliol moving on to Leiden to study under Herman Boerhaave for two years. He gained further experience in Paris at the well-known hospital of the Hotel des Invalides. Over the next ten years this young man undertook four trips across the Atlantic (it took six weeks each way) where he took part in running the family's sugar and slave interests, consolidating investments, settling difficulties after the death of his eminent father, Speaker Peter Beckford and, following the death of his turbulent older brother Peter, undertaking fundamental financial decisions on behalf of his younger brothers and sisters. His relationship with his mother Bathshua suffered when she made claim to his brother's estate and this rift took many years to heal.[1] Nevertheless, the Alderman's businesses and life prospered and he became a respected and well known member of the white Jamaican elite.

His ambition however was to be as important in the larger world of England as he was in Jamaica and to further this he involved himself in

life in London, buying a house in Soho Square. At national level he backed
a Bill to permit the direct export of sugar from the Caribbean to Europe
and saw this Bill passed by Parliament. Although he was sometimes
mocked for his Jamaican accent, he became a leading spokesman for
Caribbean affairs with a serious involvement in City of London politics,
being elected to the Billingsgate Ward of the City in 1752.[2] Now he
intended to become a country gentleman so in 1745 he bought, with the
aid of a £20,000 mortgage from Sir Jacob de Bouverie, the magnificent
estate at Fonthill, which is conveniently equidistant from London (at
that time one night's journey away) where his businesses were, from
southern English ports and from Bristol which handled some of the
slave trade.[3]

During the first few years of his ownership of Fonthill, the Alderman
improved the landscape surrounding the House, starting by opening up
the small quarry below Ashley Wood to provide the prized Chilmark
stone he needed for his building plans. His first task was to resite a
small group of village houses so that they would no longer be visible
from the house. The new village was built to the southwest, concealed
in a valley and the old village and estate church were demolished. A
new church, Holy Trinity, was built in the Grecian style, on the plan
of St Paul's Church, Covent Garden, at the top of the hill, where its
cupola could be seen from the south side of the house, enhancing the
skyline. This was completed by 1748 and consecrated by the Bishop of
Salisbury on 8 September 1749. Unfortunately the Alderman could not
be present, as he was in Jamaica again, organising the sale of two major
properties, which raised enough money to redeem the mortgage. The
Bishop led prayers for the Alderman, the service being attended by a
congregation of his tenants and employees. On his arrival at Fonthill the
Alderman had recruited musicians from his local tenantry, creating a
brass band, for which he provided uniforms. Sometimes he drilled them
himself, and no doubt they played at the consecration of his new church.
He was popular amongst the local people.[4]

Now the Alderman proposed to widen the 'serpentine' river,
created from the original Fonthill Brook, but dammed to create more
elegant lake-like proportions at its northern end. The dam could be
crossed by a footpath, below which flowed a cascade which dealt with
the overflow from the lake, a leat carrying the water back to the Fonthill
Brook as it flowed south to Tisbury. This entailed moving the public road
to the eastern side of the 'lake', and building a five arched bridge to

take the road back across the lake to its original route up the hill to join
the road from Hindon and the newly created Fonthill Gifford village
to Tisbury village road.[5] A classical temple adorned the hillside, and a
Chinese pagoda was added to the kitchen garden and orchard. At the
northern end of the newly widened stretch of water the Boat House was
created. This is in the form of a temple, with aisles, a nave and transept,
walkways in the aisles, and square piers with vermiculated capitals and
pilasters. There are semi-circular niches to each bay, and the transept
with its domed ceiling is actually a wet dock. This is likely to have been
designed by John Vardy and has been elegantly restored.

Fonthill Estate: the Boathouse by John Vardy

Beyond the bridge the lake then was narrower, but there is a
classical landing stage on the eastern side, which is so much in the
style of the boathouse and the subsequently built entrance arch that it
is tempting to attribute this to John Vardy at the same period, i.e.in the
Alderman's time. This was disputed by some historians, as the southern
end of the lake was widened later, thus making it difficult to attribute
the landing stage, with its pairs of large urns, with the now familiar
vermiculated bands, little linking wall and landing steps, to the mid
1700s. The recent discovery of drawings by the architect Papworth,

found in the RIBA collection, verify the new landing stage to be much later, after the estate was purchased by the Morrison family. All this work took place between 1745 and 1755, a time of plenty of work for the Alderman's employees and the craftsmen and labourers of Tisbury and the immediate villages. It was said of him in 1755

> who for ten years past has not paid out less than £5,000 per annum in improvements . . . whereby the poor labourers of the several neighbouring parishes have been constantly employed and their families happily supported.

Imagine the horror in the neighbourhood then, when at about one o'clock in the morning of 13 February 1755, Fonthill House caught fire. It took about an hour for help to arrive but by then it was too late to save the house. The estate workers, rudely raised from sleep, fought to save as much as possible, and managed to rescue some of the furniture, but much was lost, including William Hogarth's 'Harlot's Progress' and most of the Alderman's 'handsome' library. The Alderman, on learning of the disaster, calmly opened his desk drawer in Soho Square and announced that he had enough money to rebuild, ordering a new, even more grand house to be built by a city builder by the name of Hoare.[6]

In 1747 Joseph had met and probably married Mary Flippen, a widow who had been living in Swallowcliffe, another nearby village. Mary, born Mary Harould, had married William Flippen in Berwick St John on 31 July 1740. They lived in Tollard Royal, which is on the Dorset border, and William died in 1743 in a nearby Dorset village, Gussage All Saints. Joseph by now was 30 years old and Mary Flippen, having been married before, may have been about the same age, but her date of birth is not found amongst the English Parish Registers. Joseph and the widowed Mrs Flippen had to travel to Salisbury to obtain a Marriage Bond in order to marry, and their Bondsman is recorded as Charles Blake, a goldsmith. Permission was granted for them to marry either in St Thomas' Church in Salisbury or in the Cathedral there.[7] The reason they needed a Marriage Bond is difficult to establish. Perhaps they wanted or needed to get married quickly – it would dispense with the need for banns to be read in Church for three successive Sundays before a marriage; perhaps they wanted the privacy of a wedding in Salisbury rather than in a local village, perhaps there was family opposition to the marriage, or perhaps Mary was pregnant and they were just in a hurry to get on with it. The Bondsman, who was normally a friend or a relative, had to stand as a guarantor of a certain sum of money.

Joseph was still involved in working locally so he would have enjoyed being part of the local Tisbury community and taking part in local amusements and events. Maybe Joseph and Mary Flippen met at a local village dance, or the May Day celebrations in nearby Ansty. There had been dancing round the Maypole there for over a hundred years by the mid 1700s, with a short break during the Commonwealth under Cromwell, when music and dancing were banned. For the local community it was a chance to enjoy the pleasures of music, dancing, drinking and Springtime – perhaps to find a new girlfriend or to watch a little daughter dressed in white with ribbons and flowers in her hair, dance the steps that her mother had learnt in her girlhood. There were and are many private places in the countryside around the village of Ansty, on the way back home to Tisbury or Swallowcliffe, where perhaps a new generation of locals was conceived under the Spring stars.

Or possibly they met at a cheerfully noisy village dance in the big room of the Crown in Church Street, where the West Gallery musicians could play more loudly and much faster than they could in Church (although sometimes still the same tunes) and the beer was available at the bar. The quiet night streets of Tisbury would be disturbed but alive with noise and chatter and the sound of nailed boots on the cobbles.

But if the marriage did go ahead, there is no further mention of it in the records – either of them actually getting married, or what happened subsequently. Possibly they did not marry in Salisbury, but in Fonthill Gifford, where the church records for the period 1720 – 1760 are lost. Poor Mary, did she die in childbirth or did they fall out and never marry? However it is certainly true that in March 1748 Joseph was living in Swallowcliffe, presumably with Mary Flippen, as this is the date of the Grant to Joseph of Letters of Administration for the estate of his grandfather, Walter Lane of Chilmark, who had recently died. The Deed refers to Joseph Lane, stonecutter of Swallowcliffe. The Inventory, which should be attached the document, is missing. As 1748 is also the year in which the Stourhead Grotto was being built, perhaps Mary felt that Joseph had deserted her, leaving her alone for long periods, and the marriage, if there was an official one, broke down. Either way, she disappears from view and it is six years before Joseph finds another wife.

But life in rural Wiltshire at the time wasn't all hard work and digging the garden. There was plenty of enjoyment in the form of sports like football, single stick fighting, wrestling, bowling, cudgels, stool ball and even bull baiting, and a game called 'stobbal-play' was popular. This was played with a 3' willow bat and a ball stuffed with quills – a forerunner of cricket, perhaps. Most public revels were centred around Church Festivals, such as carol singing, with wassailing in the autumn, and mummer's plays at Christmas and Boxing Day. Shrove Tuesday brought rough games and pancakes – and perhaps the acceptance by stonemasons of a new member of their company, who had to pay 6s 8d to the warden of the company and a penny loaf and beer to other members because apprentices might only be accepted in to the company on Shrove Tuesdays. This was true in Purbeck and may also have been true in Chilmark. Stonemasons had their own particular rules and regulations. At Easter and Whit Monday there were public revels and at Rogationtide the community was involved in beating the bounds of the Parish, followed by food and drinking. The main summer event for Tisbury would be the Patronal Festival of St John the Baptist at the end of June, when games could be played on the river meadows, and there would be stalls with food, dancing and more drinking. The Morris dancers arrived, and the West Gallery band gave their clarinets, serpents and viols an airing. The Church was often the focus for socialising, even to allowing a game of fives to be played against the church walls, at the angle where the tower met the nave, but this was not always popular, as windows were broken and it cost money to repair them.

Drinking could be a problem too. Records for the local Quarter Sessions often refer to unlicensed tippling houses, unlawful gaming, drunkenness and problems with poor relief because labourers spent all their money on drink and failed to look after their families, or they fell in the river on the way home, or fights broke out. It all sounds quite normal and understandable, since life was hard and pleasures had to be taken when and where they could.

And then Joseph Lane met and married Deborah Ingram, a 23 year old young lady from Codford St Mary in Wiltshire, the wedding taking place in Tisbury in the summer of the same year – 1753 - as their son Josiah Lane was born, he being baptised in Tisbury in the September.[8] The custom at the time was that a newly married couple would, if possible, find themselves a home of their own and Joseph is always referred to as 'Joseph Lane of Tisbury', rather than of Ashley Wood, Fonthill or Fonthill Gifford. We may suppose then that Joseph, being now 36, found a cottage for himself and his family either in Tisbury village or perhaps on the road from Fonthill Gifford to Tisbury. He was now an experienced stonemason, promoted from stonecutter, having worked at Fonthill and in the Chilmark quarries, and on Alderman Beckford's new estate buildings. He had also been working at Stourhead, the experience which was to change his life for ever.

6

A JOURNEY TO WIMBORNE ST GILES

*A*lderman Beckford needs to convey his wishes to Joseph Lane. He summons his Estate Steward.

The Earl of Shaftesbury, he explains, is proposing to improve his estate at Wimborne St Giles by the addition of a Grotto, which is to be Constructed in the Rustic style, in stone, and Decorated internally with Shells. I have let the Earl know, says the Alderman, that I will be able to help with the provision of shells from the West Indies, and I also intend that Joseph shall work on the building. You will inform him that he should ready himself to travel to the Earl's Estate at Wimborne immediately.

The Steward, who knows the financial status of all the Estate workers, has the temerity to point that Joseph has no means of transporting himself, his tools, a change of clothing, a blanket or two and a canvas sheet for shelter, and Wimborne St Giles is twenty miles away. As he expects, the Alderman, who is a kind and generous- spirited employer, says – lend him a Sturdy Horse, a Welsh cob perhaps, and he can pay me back in due course.

The Alderman's gesture is not entirely selfless you understand, for although he has worked hard to become the Member of Parliament for Shaftesbury, he could not have achieved this without the support of the 4th Earl. Indeed, he had made a direct approach to the aristocrat following his failure to gain the nomination for the Penryn constituency. Shaftesbury, although he hardly knew Beckford at the time, met privately with him, they exchanged letters and after assurances from the Alderman that no financial assistance from the Earl would be needed, the Earl becomes convinced that Beckford 'has the interest of the public at heart' and so supports him in the 1747 bid for election. It is true they have common membership of the Whig party, they both mistrust the 'Pelhamite' Whigs (acolytes of Henry Pelham, brother of the 1st Duke of Newcastle),and tend to associate with anti-court figures, so much so that they were both sometimes felt to be more Tory than Whig. Shaftesbury also supports Beckford's candidacy for election as Alderman of the City of London, standing for the Billingsgate Ward.

It is unsurprising then, that the Alderman would want to be seen to help Shaftesbury with his Grotto project, being in a position to ship the requisite quantity of West Indian shells into the port of Bristol, and also to provide Shaftesbury with Joseph's growing and very useful expertise in grotto building.

The offer of the horse is speculative of course, but logical. There is no useful stagecoach service between Tisbury and Wimborne St Giles and even if there were to be one, the stage coach is a heavy, lumbering mode of transport at this time, costing 2d. or 3d. per mile plus tips to the guard and the coachman. They move at a maximum speed of four miles an hour and are uncomfortable having no springs, leather curtains and two benches for the six first class passengers inside and only a rail to hold on to for the six passengers on the top. Travelling in the basket, which hangs on the back and takes a few more passengers and the luggage, is an unpleasant ride indeed. The local carriers who go to market regularly move between villages and towns only on certain days, so useful for a trip to Hindon, or to the town of Shaftesbury, but not for cross country travel.

To get to Wimborne St Giles is a long walk across country and most hardy Englishmen who have to travel do so by means of a horse, sometimes taking along a packhorse. This is still fairly slow, but craftsmen travellers can carry their tools, food and drink, clothing and blankets and sleep outdoors rolled in the blankets under a canvas shelter. Bread, cheese and cider is sufficient for a journey, and thus the smelly, dirty and expensive inns can be avoided.

The Steward summons Joseph to his cosy Estate office and explains the Alderman's decisions. Joseph is apprehensive but pleased. How long will he be away? The Steward is unhelpful. What about his family? That will be Joseph's problem but the Steward, who is a shrewd but educated countryman is well aware of the Alderman's 'interests' in the locality and realises that

Joseph is being used to return a favour. Perhaps the Steward himself might need some assistance with a project of his own in the future – although he cannot at this stage imagine in what way this young man might be of help to him – nevertheless, the Steward recognises an opportunity and says 'You will probably be quite well remunerated for this work Joseph – perhaps a little advance to tide the family over? This can be arranged'. Joseph is both amazed and grateful. It is an example of the Alderman's goodness to his servants – a man, who, when he had to be away on business in London, left instructions to his son William to 'keep an eye on my works and my workmen' at Fonthill and referred to the necessity to earn 'the love and respect of mankind'. Not forgetting of course, that this gesture is a reciprocal arrangement which will benefit everyone, not least the Alderman himself.

Joseph clatters off across the cobbled yard to walk home to Deborah. She is naturally rather anxious at being left alone, but proud that he has been chosen for this work and can see that it can lift the family from its comparative poverty to a more comfortable life.

He collects George, the big muscly Welsh cob with hooves like feathery edged soup-plates, from the stable yard the next morning. With two canvas bags containing tools, a change of shirts and underclothes, some bread and cheese and a flask of water, blankets and a canvas sheet for shelter, Joseph sets off down Tisbury High Street, up Jobber's Lane and into Ansty village. He has a list of village names which the coachman has given him, and some primitive directions. He knows he has to keep going South, following the sun, so after riding along the lower Salisbury to Shaftesbury trackway for a while he turns left into a hollow way, up through woodland and on to the downs where he stops to look back across the Wiltshire fields and woods below and behind him. Down he goes, south into Tollard Royal, along the village road and up and away towards Sixpenny Handley, where he walks slowly though the village, riding due south again now in the afternoon sunlight. He crosses the main road from Salisbury to Blandford Forum and rides more slowly now looking around him at the Iron Age landscape – not that he could have given it such a name – but it is recognisably worked in some way he cannot yet understand. It is a long ride and he reaches the gates of the estate of the 4th Earl of Shaftesbury just before dusk. Now he is worried again – what is he to expect?

The gatekeeper at one of the lodges demands to know who he is and what is his business with the Estate and seems satisfied with Joseph's reply as he is allowed through and up the drive, reaching Riding House stableyard as instructed, where he asks for the stable manager. But he has no need to worry, the estate staff are used to itinerant additional workmen when the Earl has a Project underway, and Joseph is directed to where he can stable George, rub him down, feed and water him. After this he is to carry his saddle bags up to the hayloft above, and find a space to sleep. Joseph finds a draught free corner and a young man who is working on the building of the ornamental canal on the estate and together they go down the ladder, wash up under the cold pump in the yard and enter a huge barn where a jolly company of noisy workers are tucking into the evening meal.

Joseph is a cheerful and outgoing young man and realises that he is now part of a large itinerant group of workmen - labourers, artisans, stonemasons, gardeners, bricklayers, plasterers, joiners, and carpenters who are employed by landowners 'improving' their properties. Those working outside on the land seem to realise that the artisans working indoors are the superior workers and indeed, Joseph is interested to find that some of the craftsmen, such as the specialist plasterers are not even English, but Italian. However, everyone gets along because it is absolutely necessary to have work. Joseph will quickly become part of this pleasant, hard-working, respectable band of men, and will meet some of them again and again during the course of his life. They will get to know him and his work as he will begin to understand how the seemingly endless great expenditure on the English country houses affects all their working lives and the economy of the villages and families they are supporting.

Servant girls from the house and the dairy move amongst the men, placing on the tables great cauldrons of vegetable soup with glistening dumplings swimming in the delicious liquid. Bread and cheese is set out too. Luckily Joseph has remembered to bring his knife and a spoon, so he can tuck in. He is tired but cheerful, and tomorrow he will find out what is required of him and how he can interpret what the great Earl has in mind. He knows he is flexible, imaginative and a hard worker. He will learn from this trip and he will succeed.

Joseph and his new friend return to the hayloft, roll up in their blankets on the scratchy warm straw. He can hear the horses munching and shifting quietly below him. The face of his new wife passes fleetingly through his dreams.

The magnificent grotto at Wimborne St Giles House was constructed for the 4th Earl of Shaftesbury in 1751-1753. The owner of the estate, the 4th Earl of Shaftesbury, had sponsored Alderman Beckford when Beckford stood for the parliamentary seat of Shaftesbury in Dorset.[1]

Another connection with Joseph Lane might be deduced from the fact
that Henry Flitcroft had been commissioned in 1740-44 by the Earl to
make extensive alterations to the mid 17th century house. Perhaps he,
too, recommended the young grotto maker.

In 1754 Bishop Pococke visited and was able to note: 'a serpentine
river with an island and various decorative buildings, including a circular
pavilion dedicated to Shakespeare'. And in August 1755 Dr Evans, the
Archdeacon of Worcester Cathedral described 'a most beautiful Grotto
of the finest shells, which is said to have cost £3,000'

Wimborne St Giles: the grotto exterior

Both the Alderman and his Agent Mr John Cope had been in
correspondence with the Earl of Shaftesbury from the Beckford base
at Spanish Town in Jamaica during May and July of 1749, concerning
shipments of shells which were being arranged from the Alderman's
plantations in Jamaica.[2] Two casks of Tamarind shells would be sent on
the ships *Caesar* and *Templar* and a further third of the shells required
would arrive on the *Happy Return*.

The well known shell decorator and grotto owner 'Mr Castles of
Marylebone' had been hired to work on the interior of the Earl's new
grotto and Joseph was to work on the construction of the exterior,

which was to be in a tough, rather rugged rocky style – rocaille work - contrasting with the intricately detailed interior. Joseph would have been able to marvel at Mr Castles' way of working with shells, coral spars, ammonites and minerals, watching how he attached them to the plaster covered laths. There were plenty of decorations for Mr Castles to choose from, the Tamarinds, Venus' ear shells, conches, oyster shells and the corals. He also used coloured glass from broken wine glasses, pieces of quartz and feldspar. Large coral branches were attached to metal hooks embedded firmly in the plaster and laths and the joins covered.

The grotto is sited at the eastern end of the ornamental canal and is a free-standing building – unlike most 18th century grottoes – they tended to be built into or against a mound or slope. It is a large stone structure with a pitch-roofed inner chamber. The outer building walls are of large lumps of knobbly flint and some worked stone in the rococo style, with a rather formal entrance – double gothic style doors which open onto the first room. This arched ante-chamber is decorated with smaller flints, shells, fossils and some minerals attached to the plaster covered lath strips of the ceiling and to the side stone walls. The high walls and undulating ceiling of the inner room are fantastically covered right to the roof ridge with shells and coral branches, forming strange sea animal like shapes, trails of shiny mother of pearl shells, patterns and

Looking out from the interior of the grotto

The inner room, with shells

random shapes. The effect is one of being in a great underwater cavern. The floor is tiled (maybe installed later, as it is looks quite Victorian) and there is a small fireplace on the far wall, no doubt installed to make tea parties cosier, and to throw firelight and shadows on the decoration. Small windows allow shafts of sunlight to enter and shimmer off the pearly shell surfaces. Some of the oyster shells still contain their pearls, so the suggested cost may not be unreasonable. To each side of the entrance doors Joseph built narrow winding flint-lined tunnels, leading to the rear of the grotto, with openings in the stone to allow some light to enter.

The main grotto has been beautifully restored by the current 12th Earl of Shaftesbury, and further work is planned.

To the east of this large grotto there is a smaller grotto in a dip in the parkland, added to the park later in the 18th century or early in the 19th century.

The 4th Earl's great Rococo garden provided his visitors with more than the grotto to visit. He built cascades for the ends of his serpentine lake, an island with a castle, a 'Shake Spear's house' in which there was a bust of Shakespeare with his books housed in hanging glass fronted cases and seats on which to sit whilst studying the great author's works, a pavilion on a mound, together with a Chinese bridge and a Great Arch with twin towers.[3] A boat trip down the lake ended in the narrow canal which leads to the grotto, where tea could be taken by a warm fire. The great composer Handel was a frequent visitor, taking tea in the grotto. with his hosts.

During these early 1750s Joseph must have been able to return home occasionally, as his son Josiah was born on the 9th September 1753. He had learnt a great deal from Mr Castles, and hoped to be able to put this into practice elsewhere. Meanwhile, back home in Tisbury, a new landscape was being created.

7

FONTHILL SPLENDENS

Now there was to be more work at Fonthill, while the Alderman developed his new mansion and its picturesque surroundings. Fonthill Splendens, a wonderfully evocative name, was built on a level site to the south of the old fire damaged house, in the slightly- going-out- of- fashion Palladian style.

Once again the Alderman altered the line of the road from Fonthill Bishop to the Hindon to Tisbury road. This time it was to run to the west of the lake, providing a formal entry to the estate by an arched gateway with attached lodges, again in the Palladian style. The style is modified by the use of vermiculated bands of stone (a sort of crawling anthill tunnels design) and the use of wonderfully grumpy masks on the keystones of the arch lends it a rustic rococo feel. It is similar in style to the Triumphal Arch at Holkham Hall designed by William Kent in 1739 (finished in 1752), but Beckford's Arch is lower and more elegant with its urn finials and charming, well proportioned gate houses either side. Locally the belief is that the Arch was designed by Inigo Jones, but it is more likely to have been the work of John Vardy in about 1756, who had published a volume of engravings 'Some Designs of Mr Inigo Jones and Mr William Kent'.

The Alderman now had his grand entrance archway and drive and work proceeded on the new house. This was to be enormous, its entrance

Fonthill Estate: the Arch by John Vardy

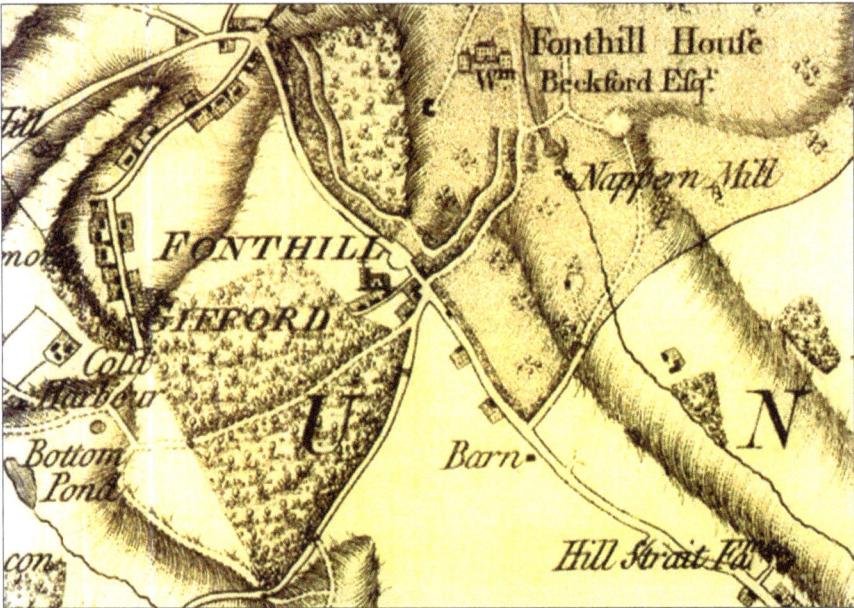

Andrews and Dury map 1773

a huge pedimented portico with four giant order columns rising above a double flight of stairs. This lead to the first, main floor which had a grand Egyptian entrance hall, paved in marble. The 'state apartments' were to the left of the hall and to the right ran a magnificent gallery for the display of the Alderman's art collection. In the basement was his library, and the rest of the house, furnished in a lavish style, reflected the grandeur of the state rooms. It was also to be a home for his family, containing items from his previous homes in Jamaica, paintings of his family and, to remind him of his origins, the doors were of Caribbean mahogany. These were not the only reminders of his Jamaican roots, as the Alderman had brought some of his Jamaican servants with him to work at Fonthill Splendens. Two huge side wings were linked to the main house by colonnades.[1] To the south the house looked up towards the ridge where the newly consecrated church stood, to the west to a wooded hill, to the north towards his classical Arch, and to the east to the serpentine river.

The building progressed rapidly, although with some setbacks. The Alderman was busy developing his 'interests' – entertaining in London, offering favours to useful contacts, finding a lucrative post for an individual or a family member, extending his patronage and always working towards gaining a secure foothold in Parliament. Polite society was extending outwards from its former tight, mostly aristocratic clique, to include powerful new City financiers, embryo industrialists and member of the arts and literary establishments – moving towards a relative equality. Alderman Beckford, for all his money and contacts, needed more. He needed the security and respectability of a wife and family. He particularly wanted a legitimate heir (he already had some eight children by his three mistresses, and although he was always kind, considerate and financially responsible towards these offspring, this was not a socially acceptable situation). He approached Maria, daughter of George Hamilton, the Member of Parliament for Wells in Somerset.[2] Her grandfather was the Duke of Abercorn, a Scottish peer, and Maria was already a widow, her husband Francis March a friend of the Alderman.

Maria was reported to be 'an agreeable lady with a large fortune' from which the Alderman would benefit and the marriage proved to be a very successful, affectionate and happy arrangement. She played an important part in advancing the Alderman's political career achievements – one very fortunate connection being her close friendship

Alderman William Beckford and Mrs Maria Hamilton Beckford

with Hester, the wife of the politician William Pitt. Maria was also good enough to accept the Alderman's existing children, as she had already had to do for Francis March's illegitimate young. On 29 September 1760 Maria produced the much wanted legitimate heir for the Alderman – William Thomas Beckford. His godfather was to be William Pitt, but unfortunately Pitt could not attend the baptism so Lord Effingham, the new baby's uncle by marriage, stood in for him.[3]

Fonthill Splendens gradually became a centre for entertaining in the fashionable current manner. Visitors included Mrs Beckford's cousin Charles Hamilton of Painshill, Lord Temple (the owner of Stowe), Elizabeth, Mrs Beckford's sister, who was Countess of Effingham together with local landowners Lord Arundell of Wardour Castle, Lord Shelburne of Bowood and the Bishop of Salisbury. It is not difficult to imagine the conversations about the new house and its developing landscape.

Now that the great entrance Archway and its lodges was in place the Alderman had decided that he needed to improve the lake and to do something about the visible scarring of the quarry face to the east, which had been further opened up to provide the building stone for the great house and now spoiled the view looking eastwards from the house.[4] Many trees would be planted, but first the lake was further widened, swamping the road on its eastern bank and ruining the Palladian bridge.

The rerouted road ran through the Arch from the Salisbury to Hindon road, past Fonthill Splendens and up to join the Hindon to Tisbury road at the top of the hill. This released the land below the quarry for planting and landscaping. Now a boat trip could be taken from the classical boathouse at the northern end of the lake, or a walk could include the newly excavated tunnel under the road to view the exciting new grottoes of the Hermit's cell and the cave. Inside the Hermit's cell, the high vaulted cavern is decorated with a sculptured relief of a reclining river god. The cell is entered by one of two low doorways and is dark and mysterious, since there are no windows. Joseph Lane is clearly responsible for the building of the tunnel and this grotto and although they are not as decorated and elegant as the Stourhead grotto, the Alderman was able to proudly conduct his friends around his newly fashionable grounds. It would seem that these early grottoes by Joseph are less likely to have been developed as part of a classically designed landscape and more as a place for pleasant enjoyment with friends.

By now Joseph was able to understand and interpret his employer's ideas. He had learned well, at Stourhead and at Wimborne St Giles and knew not only how to create and build a grotto framework (these varied from garden to garden) but also what sort of stone he might need for each stage, solid and substantial or decorative. His patrons seem to have been delighted to provide exotic decorative expensive materials. Joseph had a genius for creating magical spaces. No doubt the classical references passed him by, but he could see exactly what his patron had in mind.

At Fonthill the dating and attribution of the grottoes either side of the lake have proved contentious. There are many garden historians and many opinions. It is difficult to establish exact dates and much of the written material is, necessarily, speculative. The tunnel under the road seems to be accepted as the work of Joseph during the period the Alderman was improving his estate grounds during and immediately after the building of Fonthill Splendens. It gives accessibility from the new mansion to the south lake side. It would therefore have been excavated by Joseph between 1755 and 1760. Joseph had probably been working on the classically styled boathouse designed by John Vardy which is at the northern end of the lake. The tunnel, described by Rutter in 1823, as 'hewn in the rock' and of 'very considerable dimensions and possessing all that gloom and mystery' and a character of 'romantic magnificence', is long, winding and vaulted with smaller 'tumbler' stones already suggesting the downward pointing stalactites of Joseph's later work. It was lit by spyholes in the roof. On reaching the end, the traveller arrived in a gloomy dell, dark with yew and box trees with mysterious winding paths below sloping wooded mounds

The arched entrances to the hermitage appear below an artificial, rocky cliff, beckoning the visitor in, promising a thrilling experience – a Gothic style banquet perhaps, or a candlelit rendezvous. In the right hand cavern was a fireplace encouraging picnics, and in the left hand cavern, framed by a flint arch, was an altar with a reclining river god holding a sceptre. To the left sat Merlin, the grotto's hermit. These figures are now only just visible as shallow reliefs, but the caverns were originally highly decorated and coloured.

The tunnels and the Hermitage were referred to by the architect James Essex on a visit to Fonthill in the summer of 1766.[5] 'The Gardens are pretty . . . there is a Subterranean Grot winding 30 yards . . .The Hermitage adorn'd with Shells and Spars is well imagined.'

Robert Gemmett, in *Beckford's Fonthill*, suggests that both the tunnel and the construction of the hermitage, were elements of Alderman Beckford's plans for the Arcadian picturesque scenery to be enjoyed during a boat ride to the landing site on the other side of

The Hermit's cell and cave: Fonthill

the lake where the new plantations of beech and larch were becoming established. The hermitage had features reminiscent of Stourhead. Sadly it has now been vandalised over the two hundred and fifty years since Joseph created it.

The entrances are low, an adult needs to stoop to enter and a perceptive local Tisbury resident, Maxwell Steer, has suggested quite logically that perhaps the hermitage was built by the Alderman for his small son William.[6] Steer goes further in suggesting that the grottoes on the Eastern bank were also for William. William was born in 1760 though, so the hermitage grotto and the tunnel are unlikely to have been created for him, and by 1762 Joseph was working away from Fonthill or Tisbury.

The third creation on the western bank is the Tower, which is now an attractively crumbly ruin, but the steps to the top are clearly visible, as is the first floor room. This looks more like the work of Joseph's son, Josiah Lane, at a later date, whose cascades and grottoes were, because of the changes in taste and style in the late 1700s, more 'savagely' picturesque, more rocky, less decorated Again, this is speculative, and it is true that the tower would have been a wonderful lookout point for the Alderman's guests to see across the lake to the newly planted area under the quarry face, but there was an 'Umbrella Seat' probably on that site during the Alderman's ownership, so the Tower could have replaced this as a viewing point..

From the wooded dell the visitor could walk to a small landing stage to cross the extended lake to a footpath which led through the Alderman's new planting scheme to a grotto, which looks back westwards across the lake. This is even more difficult to date. It is clearly Lane in style, being of natural looking rock on the outside and opening via a dark tunnel into a glittering cavern of minerals, fossils, ammonites and mosaics, where water flowed gently into marble basins. It is now undecorated – because the decorative pieces have been vandalised, or did Josiah, known to have been working there as late as 1794, alter it to the savage style required by the fashionable and demanding young William?

Laurent Chatel is one historian who believes that the grottoes on the eastern bank are solely the work of Josiah.[7] He dismisses Cyrus Redding's comment that ' the East bank was ornamented with rocks, caverns, baths and grottoes in the taste of the earlier part of the century' and claims that 'the grottoes at Fonthill are entirely the work of Josiah, under the direction of William Beckford.' He cites Beckford's 1796 publication *Modern Novel Writing*, which contains a vivid description of a landscape eerily reminiscent of the east bank grottoes.

'The paths became more numerous and intricate, till they brought you to some irregular steps cut in the rock; the light stole insensible upon you as you descended; and at the foot of the steps you found the entrance of a spacious cave. All here was hushed and silent, save that the trickling drops of a purling rill struck your ear, while it softly bent its way towards the parent stream. A broken arch opened to your view the broad clear expanse of the lake, covered with numerous aquatic fowl, and weeping willows adorning its banks. Round this cave no gaudy flowers were ever permitted to bloom; this spot was sacred to pale lilies and violets. An outlet, at first scarcely perceived in the cave, carried you through a winding passage to an immense amphitheatre, formed by a multitude of irregular rocks; some bold and abrupt, others covered with ivy, periwinkles and wallflowers. One of these grottoes was destined for a bath, and ornamented with branches of coral, brilliant spars, and curious shells. A lucid spring filled a marble bason in the centre, and then losing itself for a moment under ground, came dashing and sparkling forth at the extremity of the cave,and took its course over some shining pebbles to the lake below.'

But this vivid description was in fact written in 1788 by William Beckford's half sister Elizabeth Hervey, so the grotto had been in existence for some time. Timothy Mowl comments that 'it is easy to understand how Beckford in his adolescent mystic stage, saw these grottoes as symbols of initiation; dark caverns down which the Brahmin sage Moisasour (a particularly favourite subject of young William), could lead a trusting acolyte to cleansing, or to a revelation of light and calm water' Mowl goes on to claim that the 'genially lecherous Alderman' provided the grottoes as places of entertainment for his visitors' with the surprise of sudden luxury after the gloom and that young William initially used them in exactly the same way.[8] The luxury included a cold spring water bath decorated with coral, shells and feldspar, a Chilmark stone basin, rustic seating for picnics in the lakeside grotto which was enhanced by potted roses, jasmine and orange trees, picnic food being provided on gold and silver tableware. Luxurious pleasures indeed.

So these delights could equally have been originally created by Joseph under the Alderman's direction, to please his guests, and the grotto beside the lake is particularly redolent of Stourhead, with its marble basin, and water trickling into the lake. However, the planting below and around the quarry and its caves would still have been very young, so the mystery is more difficult to imagine.

In conclusion, at this stage in the Lanes' careers, Josiah was only seven and could not have been involved to any great extent in either the tunnel, or any of the work on the grottoes at Fonthill. There had to have been a purpose for the tunnel's existence i.e. something to go and visit at the end of it, both on the western bank (the hermitage) and, if a landing stage on the eastern bank was built around this time, it is likely that there was something to visit there too. Certainly Josiah is known to have continued working at Fonthill later on, in the 1780s and 90s, and much more 'rockifying' was to occur at the behest of William when these young boys became adults, but by that time tastes and fashions in gardening had changed irrevocably.

A compelling reason to assert that Joseph built both the hermitage and grottoes on the lakeside, is that Charles Hamilton, having heard about Joseph's work at Fonthill, must have wished to see this remarkable work before he requested that Joseph come and create his proposed magical grotto at Painshill.

8

MEETING MR BROWN

Joseph's family had increased during the 1750s and early 1760s. Josiah, born in 1753, was joined by a sister Deborah, baptised on 8 May 1755. Sadly, although Joseph and Deborah had three more babies, the next two, little girls, Rebecca born 1759 and Tabitha born 1763, both died during the first year of life. Another sister, Rebeckah, was born in 1765.[1] So Josiah and Deborah were still young children when Joseph left home to start work on the cascade at Loakes Manor at the request of William, the 3rd Earl of Shelburne, yet another friend of the Alderman.

The 3rd Earl had just inherited Loakes Manor, at High Wycombe, and had requested Mr Lancelot 'Capability' Brown to redesign the grounds. It is possible that Humphrey Repton was also involved at Loakes, but at a later date. The grounds were improved to include an icehouse, a ha-ha, the lake, a cascade and a grotto and it was to create the cascade that Joseph Lane was employed. Curiously, Joseph's lifespan almost exactly matches that of Capability Brown (1716-1783). (Joseph was born in 1717 and died in 1784.) Brown designed The Dyke at Loakes, a long, narrow stretch of water which is crossed by the drive. At the end of

The Dyke is the cascade, where the water level drops about five metres to its natural level.

John Britton and Edward Wedlake Brayley, writing in 1818 in *Introduction to the original delineations . . ..intituled [sic] The Beauties of England and Wales* mentions that Loakes Manor House is about to be renovated by James Wyatt.[2] They add that the front of the house

> is rendered pleasant by a spacious sheet of water, which winds through the grounds for nearly three quarters of a mile and is terminated by a small artificial cascade executed by the ingenious Mr J Lane and claiming admiration for its variety of parts and picturesque effect.

It has been suggested that the cascade is the work of Josiah Lane, but Josiah was only nine years old in 1762, and garden historian Mike Cousins places the building of the cascade as occurring during that year.[3] There is also a grotto in the grounds, not, as had become usual, facing the lake, but situated at the foot of the cascade, where the natural water level is resumed and although there is no specific mention of this being the work of Mr J Lane it certainly seems likely. It was filled in during the second half of the 20th century and it is now impossible to see inside, as the grotto has been blocked with flint. It is just possible to see where it is, as the outline of the right side wall is just visible below the growth

Loakes Manor, High Wycombe: grotto and cascade in 1920

The cascade, showing the now blocked up grotto

of tangled ivy which covers the stonework. From the photograph taken during the 1930s it certainly looks like a Lane grotto.

The cascade however, still flows elegantly over Joseph's natural looking stone waterfall, trickling down into a clean stream bed, which is now edged with a small gravel beach and some marshy planting further downstream. The area is much used by walkers, cyclists and runners who circuit Capability Brown's serpentine lake.

Imagine Joseph arriving at the Loakes Manor estate after the very long ride from Tisbury, probably riding up from Hindon and along the Ridgeway, passing Warminster and Marlborough, turning due east towards the River Thames, Reading and then north to High Wycombe, taking two or three days to complete the journey. The Earl's Estate Steward introduces him to a gentleman of his own age, simply dressed in a dark brown jacket, with a kind, quizzical expression on his face. ' This is Mr Lancelot Brown,' says the steward. 'He will explain to you what is required.' Mr Brown takes Joseph into the estate grounds, pointing out the work he has planned and which is underway, the damming of the stream to form a long serpentine lake, the new plantings he has ordered. At the south eastern end of the new lake, he explains, will be the dam and then it will be possible to take the water down the necessary drop of twenty feet or so, to flow onwards as the original stream.

A cascade is to be built by Joseph, and where it becomes the stream again, Joseph is to build a grotto into the side of the hill. A Natural Feature is what the third Earl wants, although Mr Brown has not yet told him so, so that the Family and Friends may walk the length of Mr Brown's new lake, amongst his newly planted shrubs and trees, and discover a set of mossy steps beside the cascading water. They may descend, and sit in contentment in the shelter of the grotto to view the parkland to the east and north – views of the Parish Church and the hills. 'Serendipity' says the cheerful Mr Brown, 'is what we are looking for, the happiness of finding an unexpected pleasure – your cascade and grotto my dear Mr Lane'.

No elaborate decorations are required for the grotto interior, just simple natural stone, perhaps some ammonites, and a stone seat, natural woodland – just a fortuitously lovely secluded place to sit and contemplate, with the curve of the hillside behind you, the trees casting a green and sensuous shade, the sound of the water cascading down the stones and the clear stream sparkling in the sun. Serendipity indeed.

9

THE CHANGING VILLAGE

Josiah and Deborah Lane were nine and seven when Joseph left Tisbury to work at Loakes Manor. They may have been lucky enough to be among the poor children of the parish of Tisbury who benefitted from the Will of Alice Coombes, an unmarried lady from Chicksgrove, who,when she died in 1731, left £400 to be used for the poor children of the Parish 'for the teaching of them to read'. The children of Chicksgrove and Hatch were also to benefit. Twenty-six children attended the school at any one time and learned to read through the kindness of Alice Coombes but it is not known in which house the teacher lived, where classes were held. There is a cottage half way down the upper High Street in Tisbury known as The Old School House and further research might reveal whether this was in fact the teacher's house, the number of children and their names. The lucky ones attended from the age of four until they were ten and children, having learned to read and follow Church teachings and the Bible, could go onto learn some arithmetic if parents supplied ink and paper.[1] On the first day of Lent an examination was held, testing reading the Bible and reciting the catechism.

By the mid 1760s Joseph's parents Thomas and Sarah were more than middle aged, in fact for the period, they would have been considered quite old. Again it is difficult to establish when and where they died, but the death of a Thomas Lane is recorded at Gillingham in February 1739 when Thomas would have been 59.[2] The records for Fonthill Gifford parish for the mid 1750s are lost, so Thomas and Sarah might have died at Fonthill - no dates are available. Life tended to be short and difficult in the Georgian period and the records for many lives remain untraceable. Ownership of Fonthill had changed from the Cottington family to the Beckford family, and although Alderman Beckford was known for his kindness to his employees, when they became old or ill, and could not work, the cottage would be needed for a new worker. Thereupon the old ones moved out, to the care of the family, or to poor relief provided by the parish or to the workhouse.

Along the lane from the newly created village of Fonthill Gifford, the new church had as its neighbour the Beckford Arms. Passing the crossroads there were scattered small stone and thatched cottages on the south side of the road, built about 100 yards apart. Each of these cottages is set sideways on to the road, in the same practical style as many European, eastern European and Russian village houses. The house thus faced its own yard with a vegetable garden behind it, perhaps a small outbuilding or two and probably a small amount of land. Now the Enclosure Acts started to take away not only the little piece of land with each cottage, but worse, the cottagers right to graze animals on the common spaces behind the cottages. This, as mentioned before, did improve the national agricultural return in the form of more bushels of corn per acre, but forced the villagers to live without a house cow, or sheep or a couple of pigs. Diets began to deteriorate, bread from wheat now having to be bought, no cow to provide milk so no cheese or butter and the pig would have to be housed in the outbuilding and be fed scraps. Vegetable broth from garden root crops, peas and beans, was a staple with the bread, and any meat that could be afforded, infrequently, had to be boiled or fried, as most people did not have an oven. Beer and cider were available, and being inebriated a common condition, as well it might be since other comforts and amusements were sparse. In Tisbury there were probably three watering places – the Boot, the Crown, and the Cross. The Crown which is the oldest inn, it is said was built at the request of the parishioners of St John the Baptist, the parish church, who had to travel on foot to church on Sundays, sometimes from quite a long way away, and requested a place of refreshment.[3]

It is hard to emphasise sufficiently the effect of the Enclosures on normal country people; the change may have been gradual but it was a slow disaster affecting many families, particularly the loss of the grazing rights. The price of food rose during the second half of the century, but wages failed to keep up, and in fact, fell. Many of the poorer families suffered considerably, ending up in the workhouse, or if they were lucky, in receipt of Poor Relief. Land which was enclosed around Tisbury included Teffont Common, Chilmark Common, land to the south around Wardour, and land around Fonthill. Here a wall was built a little later by young William Beckford to keep his new Fonthill Abbey grounds secluded and private, which included parish common land such as Lords Common to the NW of Fonthill Gifford, Coxes' Common west of Stops Beacon and a large area known as Tisbury Common between Stops Beacon and Upper and Lower Lawn Farms, all clearly marked on Andrews and Dury's map of 1773. By 1838 there was no common land left around Tisbury.

The parish workhouse was at the eastern end of the churchyard of St John the Baptist, Tisbury. The costs of keeping the poor in the workhouse were born by the parish, as was poor relief – the sums paid out by the Parish Overseer to those in need. This money was raised as a tax from landowners and the more fortunate villagers – not a popular tax, but one which everyone understood to be necessary – who knew who might be the next person needing a word with the Overseer?[4]

Next door to the workhouse, the Church was in regular use, but in 1762, following previous damage, the 60ft spire was struck by lightning and fell down, crashing through the North Transept roof and into the aisle. Luckily no-one was hurt and the six bells remain undamaged. Work was started to replace the damaged upper stage of the tower by constructing a superstructure tower with battlements, but no spire.[5] Mr Thomas Osmond was commissioned to provide a single dial clock. No doubt the local stonemasons were delighted that the Crown inn was so close, as it was thirsty work hauling stone up the scaffolding. The incumbent at this time was William Thomas, who had followed the Rev. Thos. Marchant. The Patron was Tabitha Marchant of Hatch. Hence the popularity of the name Tabitha in Tisbury.

By now there were more cottages either side of the upper part of the High Street, from Hindon Lane at Hill Street Farm, down to the junction of the lane to Tuckingmill where the bend in the High Street led down what is now known as the Causeway and took the road towards Church Street. There were cottages along Cuffs Lane, Duck Street, Court Street as far as Place Farm, and Church Street, where the road ended at the Crown, where fields stretched away up the hill.

Tisbury had been a wealthy and busy parish as early as the 1300s, although the Black Death in 1349 had affected the village very badly (75 Tisbury Manor tenants alone died and this number did not include their families or their workers). No burial site for the victims of the Black Death is formally identified, but the large area in the western corner of the churchyard is completely bare of tombstones and the height of the ground reaches nearly to the top of the surrounding stone wall. This seems to indicate that it was a filled area and it is at the farthest point from the church itself and from the river. By 1370 the village was a substantial tax paying community again – there were 433 poll tax payers recorded in 1371.[6] By the end of the 18th century the population had grown to 1,961 souls and by 1831 it had become 2,259 people.

For those in work in the 18th century, goods could be bought in various places. Not many shops seem to have been available but pedlars arrived on foot, selling small items such as ribbons and lace, needles and pins, old books and small items of clothing, trinkets and bonnets. Hawkers, who had a horse and a cart or waggon sold tinware such as buckets, saucepans, skillets, knives etc.

At nearby Hindon, which was sited at the junction of south Wiltshire's main roads east to west and south to north, there was a regular weekly market, said to be the second largest corn market in Wiltshire (which had twenty markets at the time). Hindon's market could be reached either by walking or by the local carrier, and here it was possible to buy food such as poultry, butter, fish, cheese, linens, thread and wool or yarn, leather goods, hops, meat, as well as corn, sheep, horses, and cattle. Ironware, candles, brooms and salt were also on sale. The main street, lined with houses on either side was wide enough for the tenants of the houses to erect stalls in front of their homes.[7] Behind the houses lay plots where they grew the produce they sold each week. These houses were built with thatched roofs and in the Great Fire of Hindon, in 1754, virtually all the High Street houses were destroyed. Of the fourteen inns and public houses, only one survived.[8] Hindon was rebuilt in the local stone, with its wide street retained so that the weekly market could continue. Hindon also had two annual fairs, which were much bigger events, one on the Monday before Whitsun and the autumn one on the 29th October each year. Hindon was known as a 'pocket borough', electing two members of Parliament. The father of the well-known parliamentarian Charles James Fox, was Henry Fox, who became an MP for Hindon in 1734. Another curious fact is that in 1748 the Duke of Newcastle owned a small property in Hindon High Street, just down from the main west to east road at its High Street junction and almost opposite the Lamb Inn. Both Charles James Fox and the Duke of Newcastle were to influence the lives of the Lane family.

Salisbury had its market on Tuesdays, and by leaving early enough it was possible to get there and back in a day by the local carrier's cart. Nearby Shaftesbury also had a market, which blocked the main west road through the little town and caused minor riots from time to time. Shaftesbury also had a butter cross, a market house where the town weights and measuring scales were kept and used, and no fewer than twenty-four inns, which were in great demand.

Annually there was a huge fair at Weyhill in Hampshire, but that was far away from Tisbury, and unlikely to attract many villagers although it was an important hiring fair where workers could advertise themselves as easily identifiable shepherds, milkmaids, cowmen or labourers and find employment for the whole of the following year. It must have taken some courage to travel so far away to try and obtain new employment. Apparently you could also sell your wife there, though this must have been quite difficult to arrange, particularly if the wife did not want to go.

For the traveller who had money however, it was now possible to travel east to London or west to Exeter by one of the six stagecoaches which left Salisbury each week. By 1770 there twenty-four departures each week as the journey became easier with the turnpiking of the roads. Until turnpiking (which started in the Salisbury area in 1753), each parish was required to elect two parishioners to act as Highway Surveyors or Waywardens. These gentlemen inspected the roads, the watercourses, bridges and pavements of the parish three times a year, reporting all the work which needed to be done to maintain the parish road system. Any person who owned land valued at £50 p.a. had to supply two men, their working tools, horses and wagons for a number of consecutive days a year (initially four, then six) and these workmen were expected to keep the roads, watercourses, and bridges in good repair. This system was open to abuse on all sides and failed to keep the parish roads in any state of repair at all.[9] Quite often there were long stretches between parishes for which no-one would admit responsibility. It was certainly more comfortable to walk, avoiding the ruts and the potholes, or to ride on horseback, than to travel on a cart or even in a stagecoach. So when the turnpike system was introduced, it was recognised as a necessary, but evil alternative. Turnpike Trusts were set up privately to run a stretch of road with toll gates and toll houses installed where 'turnpikers' could stop all traffic and collect the imposed tolls. These tolls would then be used to repair and maintain and even improve the roads. The tolls varied from area to area, but for example, for each horse pulling a stagecoach a charge of three pennies could be made. For each horse pulling a cart, two pennies; a horse being ridden, one penny. A score of oxen merited five pennies and a score of sheep tuppence ha'penny. It was not always successful – toll gates were broken, and occasionally toll houses were burned down by irate mobs; travel at night was a problem as the toll keeper or turnpiker had to be woken to allow through traffic.[10] It was considered an unfair system but long distance roads in particular improved, and by 1784 the new, fast, mail coaches were able to provide a reliable carrying system for both mail and passengers.

10

CHARLES HAMILTON COMES TO DINNER –
AND JOSEPH TRAVELS TO SURREY

*M*rs Maria Beckford has invited the Hon. Charles Hamilton to visit *Fonthill Splendens. The Alderman is delighted to be able to show Charles his palatial new house and its improved surroundings. Charles, as he alights from his carriage, is suitably impressed by the double external staircase, the massive columns and his warm welcome from the Beckfords as they usher him in to the Egyptian Hall. He admires the murals by Andrea Casalis and the new magnificent organ which replaces the one burned in the fire.*

They progress formally around the house, giving Charles time to view the Gobelin tapestries, the state bed, the gallery with the Alderman's picture collection and the well stocked basement library. Charles, who has already completed two Grand Tours, expresses his amazement and admiration. He is privately pleased that his cousin Maria is so handsomely settled.

Dinner is served in the formal dining room hung with its family portraits. It is of course, a lavish meal – the Alderman is rightly proud of the game he raises for sport on the estate- there is always something in season, pheasant, duck, snipe, woodcock. The household is never short of sugar or spices, so desserts are always rich and delicious. The wine is imported – claret and dessert wines from Bordeaux, port from Portugal and of course

Fonthill Splendens (above) and The Hon. Charles Hamilton (below)

rum from the Jamaican estates. The Alderman's black servants behave impeccably and dinner is a relaxed and jolly occasion.

A walk afterwards is clearly needed and the two men set off around the grounds, stopping at the colonnaded boathouse to board a rowing boat. They set off down the lake to view the new tree planting scheme on its eastern bank and alight on the other side to view the hermitage and to walk through the dark and mysterious tunnel under the road, back to the house. The Alderman mentions his hunting lodge, the temple and his new church.

Back in the library, the Alderman offers Charles a glass of claret or Jamaican Rum.

"Claret for me please" replies Charles, arranging the skirt of his scarlet frock coat carefully on the wide library chair. He is keen to discuss his own

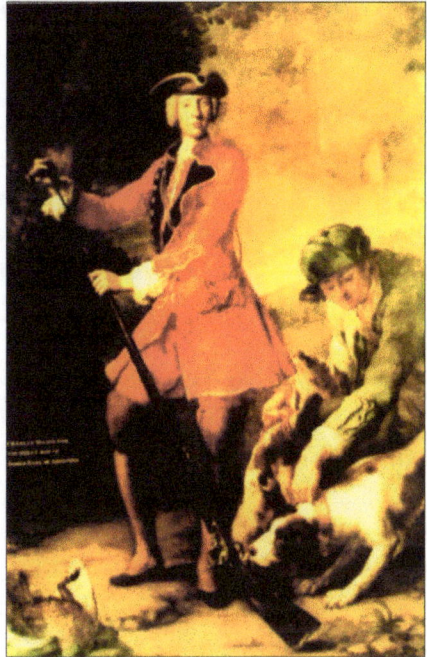

garden plans with his host, talking about his last European tour, the purchase of the Painshill Estate in Surrey and his proposals for the future of the great garden he is constructing there.

"I am already pumping water from the River Mole to form the lake, and have created islands and bridges. The Abbey ruin is underway and I am planning a vineyard on the south facing hill above the lake – I shall plant Pinot Noir grapes so that we will produce a sparkling wine" he says confidently. "It will rival all the French wines". The Alderman is amused – he likes Charles' enthusiasms, many of which he shares.

"I am planning a Gothic temple, a tower, a Turkish tent and all sort of delights. Now I find that simply everyone is talking about grottoes, so I shall have to build one. It will be the centrepiece of the whole journey around the garden, a place full of light and shadows, precious stones and shimmering water. The visitor will cross a bridge and come upon it as if by lucky chance. I saw many grottoes in Italy, but mine will be more magical." He is clearly carried away by the whole idea.

An idea strikes the Alderman and he makes a bold suggestion – "My dear Charles" he says, settling himself more comfortably upon the rather rigid brocaded sofa - "One of my estate staff, Thomas Lane who is himself a stonemason, has a son, Joseph who has been working for Henry Hoare at Stourhead on his grotto and for Shaftesbury down at Wimborne St Giles – I believe that young Joseph may be just the man for your new grotto. He's learned his trade well, working successfully, I understand, under Henry's architect Flitcroft, and is a strong, keen worker and an excellent stonemason. May I suggest, Charles, that you arrange for Joseph to visit Painshill at your leisure and undertake some of the grotto work, if not all of it?"

Charles is already well aware of Joseph Lane's work, and as this was his plan anyway, he is glad the Alderman has made the suggestion.

"Indeed, sir, I shall be delighted to offer your man Joseph employment. I can arrange for his accommodation in the village near Painshill and he may arrange to arrive as soon as he wishes"

The following day Joseph is summoned to Fonthill Splendens and appraised of the gentlemen's plans for him. He is to travel with the carrier to Salisbury, then to Andover, Basingstoke and through Guildford towards Cobham and Painshill. The Alderman, who is known for his kindness to his workers, arranges for an eye to be kept upon Deborah and the children until Joseph has earned some money at Painshill and can return for a visit. It is all decided. There is no choice – Joseph's fate is sealed.

By the time Joseph arrived at Painshill, the garden was already more than a sparsely planted building site, but a garden only in the imagination of the Hon. Charles Hamilton. Charles was the fourth son of the Earl of Abercorn, born in 1704, and often short of funds. This was no impediment to his ideas; he was always noted for the inspirational advice he gave to his friends on estate improvement. In 1738, after he had travelled across Europe on two Grand Tours, he was able to lease 400 acres of hilly heathland at Painshill, Cobham in Surrey and fulfil his dream of an Elysian garden of his own.[1] There was no main house but by 1748 Horace Walpole was able to comment that Hamilton had achieved 'a fine place out of a most cursed hill'. Hamilton had connections with the 3rd Earl of Shelburne, and with Henry Hoare 'the Magnificent' of Stourhead – he banked with Hoare's bank from 1747 and they exchanged gardening ideas and opinions. In 1750 Hamilton's youngest daughter Sarah had married Kenton Couse, the architect Henry Flitcroft's assistant and pupil, so once again the careers and lives of Joseph and Josiah Lane, were helped and driven by the tight social and family connections around Alderman Beckford.

Nearly twenty years of landscaping and planting had occurred in Hamilton's garden before Joseph saw Painshill. Some of the structures were in place, but although the park was still incomplete, Charles' interpretation of a landscape painting by Poussin was much admired. The creation of a grotto was to be a masterpiece, and although it took many years, great costs and the building of it was interrupted by a period of lack of money, the final result was, and again now is, a place of enchantment, of magical, shimmering light. Charles seems to have wanted more glitter, more theatre than the mythological or classical effects achieved at Stowe and at Stourhead. But it was to be a coherent concept, unlike Pope's eclectic mixture at his grotto in Twickenham. Gardening styles were already moving on, less Virgilian in inspiration and more savagely picturesque - more rocks, less glitter, but not at Painshill, or subsequently Oatlands Park and Ascot Place where the Lanes' work represents the apogee of the highly decorated, theatrical grotto.

At Painshill the grotto is approached on the visitor circuit through the Alpine Garden, past the vineyard, the delightful ogee Gothic temple, down to the Abbey ruin and along the lakeside to a Chinoiserie bridge. This crosses a narrow channel in the lake and deposits the visitor on an island, slightly wooded, with an apparently rocky crest, a crown of

The entrance to the Painshill grotto

jagged stone. The island is in two halves, a narrow stream between them being crossed by a wide stone and turf bridge, the stone being spongestone, holey and pitted and sometimes known as tufa. Below the arch nestles the grotto, invisible from above. At the end of the arch, a lawn slopes gently down to a further bridge – the grass almost covered by a magnificent Cedar of Lebanon. The second bridge would take the visitor to the other side of the lake and on to the mausoleum and the Turkish tent, but by retracing his steps, passing the cleverly designed rocky spongestone outcrops, built by Joseph to look as natural as possible, the visitor reaches the entrance to the grotto. The tunnel passageway is 60 feet long, and eventually reaches a chamber 36 feet across, with a large central support column. Joseph and the men he must have had working with him, built a solid brick core with timber roofing covered in lead. This roof in turn was earthed, turfed and planted with shrubs. The bricks were made in a small brickworks nearby, behind the ' Abbey ruin'. The exterior sides of the grotto are artfully covered in the skull like spongestone rock, brought from Daglingworth near Cirencester, and from Combe Down and Widcombe quarries close to Bath and Joseph placed these rocks so that the visible parts of the grotto appeared to be a natural cavern in the island.[2]

The initial work at Painshill lasted from 1762-1765, when sadly for Charles Hamilton and all his workers, the money ran out, and the workers were paid off and temporarily dismissed.

It was at this point that Joseph had to return home to Tisbury, having received a payment, on 16 January 1764 of £343 2s. 10d., this being for, probably, his work on the framework of the building.[3] How did Deborah and the two children manage in Tisbury if this was the first payment? Mike Cousins, garden historian, reports that Hamilton hired Joseph for £40 per annum from 1763 and that this information came from Norman and Beryl Kitz' book of 1984 –Pains Hill Park; Hamilton and his Picturesque Landscape. However, the Kitz' provide no evidence of this annual payment, and even if Joseph did receive £40 per annum from 1763 onwards, how did Deborah manage for the first year? Did she and the children travel up to Painshill to live there with Joseph? This seems very unlikely as baby Tabitha was born, baptised and also died in Tisbury in 1763 and the next baby, Rebeckah, was born in 1765, again in Tisbury. It seems more likely that Joseph was able to travel home very occasionally during the initial Painshill building period of 1762-5 and Deborah managed on her own.

View of the grotto from the far side of the lake

There is also the question of Joseph's living and travelling costs. Perhaps there was a system of advancements against final payments. Another question that arises is, did the first payment of £342 2s. 10d. have to cover the cost to Joseph of assistance from other workers? The approximate weekly wage of a labourer at this time was about 9s. per week – less than £25 per annum, so if the £342 had to cover two years' work, 1762 and 1763, paying two labourers say £30 p.a. each (£120) this would leave Joseph with £122 p.a. for himself, or about £2 6s. 8d. per week – an excellent wage for a working stonemason at that time.[4] It does seem possible then, that Joseph paid for his own labouring assistants, as he would have needed strong men to handle stone, planks, lead, pulleys and winches and wooden wheelbarrows full of crystals during the work on the interior. Charles Hamilton would have provided the brick, the lead, the decorative crystals etc but the Lanes had to know where they came from, how best to use each type of stone or quartz and how to work, flake and fix every single piece.

At least Joseph was now earning a decent wage and also learning how to cover his costs both at work and in Tisbury. He may even have been thinking about buying a cottage and making some financial provision for his growing family.

II

AT CASTLE HILL – EVOLVING A STYLE

In 1766 Joseph started work on a grotto in Dorset, at Castle Hill, Duntish near Buckland Newton (now known as Duntish Court). He was probably recommended for this work by the architect William (not yet Sir William) Chambers, known as 'Chinese' Chambers for his visit to China with the Swedish East India Company, and his books about Chinese and Oriental gardening and architecture. William Chambers had designed the 'Chinese' bridge linking the Painshill grotto island to the main garden and was therefore aware of Joseph's growing expertise. Chambers, who helped found the Royal Academy in 1768 became Comptroller of the King's Buildings after Henry Flitcroft and a very fashionable architect. He built Somerset House, amongst many other important commissions, and when the King of Sweden knighted him, George III granted that this knighthood be recognised in Great Britain too.

Castle Hill built in 1764, for Fitzwalter Foy, was a comparatively small private commission.[1] The building was a handsome, square, red brick classically styled house, with stone details, two side wings, the southern one containing the servants' bedrooms above a brewery and a laundry, and the northern wing providing stables and a coach house. Inside, the house had beautiful plasterwork including a ceiling in the main drawing room decorated with plaster musical instruments. The doorcases were all finely detailed and very handsome and the house had an elegant oak staircase. The basement provided a servants' hall, kitchen and scullery, cellars, butler's and housekeeper's rooms.

The estate garden lay below the plateau on which the house was built, and from the large raised ground floor windows and beyond the ha-ha stretched the patchwork of the Dorset countryside, tier by tier down to the flat land and then up to Dungeon Hill and North Dorset. To the south and west William Chambers had planted specimen trees and shrubs including a ginkgo biloba from China, which today is the second largest gingko in Britain. Gravelled walks led down to an ornamental brick lined canal and William suggested a grotto and cascade amongst the trees, the grotto to be set into the steep terraced bank.

An awkward journey to the village of Duntish for Joseph, and this time he feels that Josiah at thirteen is quite old enough to accompany him and start to learn the increasingly valuable trade and art of grotto building. The distance is about 26 miles today, but in 1766, taking into account the lack of direct roads and because they were sharing a horse and carrying tools and clothes, much longer. Joseph and Josiah would have left Tisbury, to ride North and then West, crossing the Ridgeway and climbing on much higher past Mere and Stourhead and then turning south towards Stalbridge where they could link up with the old Sherborne Road towards Dorchester, which passes quite close to Duntish. It would certainly be a couple of days slow travelling and over some long stretches of isolated trackway.

As the house was by now completed, father and son were probably housed in the stable block in the north wing. Joseph had ideas for this grotto, as Charles Hamilton had shown him pictures of real caves with what looked like hanging icicles, and had allowed him to handle some incredibly beautiful pieces of rock, amethyst with its purple and lilac geometric pyramids, pink and white rose quartz, and a wonderful smooth, rounded stone broken in half which when opened looked like sparkling white caverns, with sharp stalactites pointing down from miniature ceilings. If only one could walk into such a cavern, what a thrill that would be thought

A split geode showing interior crystals

Castle Hill, Duntish, Dorset: the grotto exterior

Joseph. He could create an interior like that, he thought. This grotto at Castle Hill would be a test of his ability and could help with the lavish decoration he intended for the interior of Charles Hamilton's Painshill grotto.

The outer shell of Castle Hill would, however, be quite rustic, constructed of quite large boulder like stones and flints with a short entrance tunnel, lit by small apertures and leading to a substantial inner chamber, where he would be able to construct a plunge pool. This would refill itself from a spring to the side, and also from natural intermittent rainwater, which it still does today. No pump is involved. The wall at the back lining the bank is now sadly deteriorated but the present owner, whose family have lived on and owned the site for some generations, has repaired a great deal of the inner stonework, making it safe again.

The interior decoration still needs considerably more expensive restoration but what is visible as a result of the deterioration, is Joseph's building systems, the little bricks he used, the lath and plastered cones and what would seem to be his first use of decorative flakes of feldspar. This was to be his first attempt at his signature decorative style of overlapping stone and jewel-like flakes of feldspar in patterns and swirls and it is possible to see how he has worked out how to attach his 'stalactites' to the ceiling. He has made different sized cones of laths covered in canvas and coated with plaster, to which he has laboriously attached layer upon layer of coloured feldspar flakes, small thinly split pieces of the feldspar. He then hangs these cones on to firmly placed metal hooks in the brick and plaster ceiling, after which he works more small pieces of the feldspar into the plaster, covering the joins between cones and ceiling until the stalactites hang smoothly down from above, their fixing invisible.

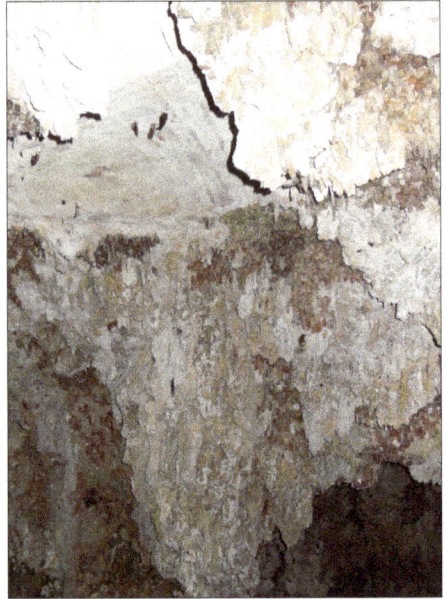

Interior at Castle Hill grotto, showing the stalactite support hooks

Josiah in his turn was learning. Fetching, carrying stone, splitting oak for the laths, handing the right pieces to his father, splitting feldspar, sorting colours, learning to apply plaster to the cones, and watching his father spontaneously designing. It was, for both of them, slow, back-breaking hard work. Every stone had to be moved, put in the right position, made safe and firm and look right. Although some light came in through the planned apertures, it could be dark and cold in a grotto, and sometimes a very solitary occupation. Did Josiah want to do this for the rest of his life? Later on he is reported as being 'the taciturn Mr Lane' but perhaps he was just a quiet, hard- working lad, with no other real option but to work with his father. At least they were comparatively well paid, better than labourers, even if not yet on a par with say, an Italian plaster craftsman. In addition there wasn't much chance of spending the money while working away from home on a remote rural estate. Castle Hill at least had its own brewery and cellars, so it is possible that evenings with other workers, and the young house maids and estate staff might be very jolly.

Below the grotto lies the canal, where there is evidence of a cascade at the western end nearest the grotto site. Attempts have been made to restore this but it is now again overgrown and not working as a cascade, since it needs a pumping system. Perhaps it was originally a Lane cascade, since they were working within yards of the site of it and Joseph had not long finished the Loakes Manor cascade. The stones are now largely dispersed, the site overgrown and virtually invisible.

Castle Hill House in 1830 became the venue for one of the 'Captain Swing' riots, when agricultural labourers in the South of England revolted against the use of threshing machines, which denied them their extra winter wages. Curiously Tisbury too was one of the main sites of revolt, but none of the labourers at either venue benefitted from their small revolution and many of them were either imprisoned or transported for life.[2]

On the site of Castle Hill House now stands the present owner's large comfortable single storey home. The old house was sold in 1840 and allowed to gradually decline, one owner even selling off the lead for the roof, and thus allowing even faster deterioration. In 1965 the house was demolished and the new building erected. The current owners have planted sensitively, replanted where necessary and restored the grounds where possible. They have surrounded the new house with a magnificent wisteria, covering the walls during the early summer months. A large and imposing magnolia grandiflora dominates the entrance courtyard and in the grounds the old gingko biloba continues its splendid life, together with a large handkerchief tree (davidia involucrata), other specimen trees, camellias and azaleas, all flourishing in the soft woodland soil. 'Chinese' Chambers would be happy to see his landscaping surviving the centuries, and no doubt Joseph and Josiah would be glad to know their grotto is still visited and appreciated.

12

CLAREMONT PARK

The creation of a grotto as an embellishment to the landscape garden reached its peak between the 1750s and 1790s. Some landowners even indulged in more than one grotto and Henry Pelham-Clinton the 9th Earl of Lincoln and subsequently the 2nd Duke of Newcastle was one of these richly fortunate gentlemen. Reputed to be the most handsome man in England, Henry had been accompanied on his Grand Tour by his very close friend Horace Walpole. On his return from studying fencing in Turin, Italy, and after a spectacular quarrel with Walpole, Henry came home to marry his cousin Catherine Pelham, daughter of the then Prime Minister Henry Pelham, who also happened to be the younger Henry's Uncle. This resulted in Henry becoming the heir to both Uncle Henry Pelham and to his other uncle, the Duke of Newcastle. By special remainder granted by George II, Henry became the 2nd Duke of Newcastle–under-Lyme, in 1768.

Whilst still the 9th Earl of Lincoln during the 1750s, Henry 'improved' the family property at Claremont Park in Esher, Surrey. Claremont, bought by the Pelham family from the architect, spy and playwright Sir John Vanbrugh, already possessed elegant landscaped grounds, including the large Ampitheatre, a series of semi-circular terraces overlooking the lake, designed in 1722 by Charles Bridgman for Thomas Pelham, the 1st Duke of Newcastle. There had been a cascade in the grounds by 1733, a Palladian style structure, but in 1750 a Grotto was installed for Henry by a Hyde Park stonemason, Joseph Pickford senior. This Joseph was the father of the better known Joseph Pickford, architect. He was working under the direction of designer Stephen Wright, a pupil of William Kent, and some time in June 1750 one Colonel James Pelham a family member, reported to the 1st Duke of Newcastle that

> at the Grotto the arches are got twelve foot high.[1] He (Pickford) talks of 'getting some Glass cinders to mix with inside'. By the end of June 'they (had) fix'd al the great Stones at the Rock, which is a fine thing' and an evergreen plantation was being planted behind the Grotto.

The same year saw a report from Colonel Pelham of a visit to Claremont by 'the Two Mr Beckfords that are brothers to my Lady Effingham, commenting that

> one has a Plantation in Jamaica, his Seat here is I think in Wiltshire where he is making fine Gardens &c. I never see a Man in Such Extacies as he was with Claremont, they were all prodigiously pleased with everything![2]

In 1754 the Fulham tapestry manufactory made a magnificent tapestry panel showing the Grotto, the Belisle Garden Pavilion and a number of delightful exotic birds from the Duke's Claremont menagerie. To this day there are tame black swans on the lake. The exterior of the Grotto shown on the panel looks very similar to its exterior today.

In 1760 a book by a Mrs Joel-Henrietta Pye (although it is said it may really have been written by her husband James Pye), Mrs Pye describes *A Short view of the Principal Seats and Gardens in and about Twickenham*. Mrs Pye visits a number of properties, among them Oatlands Park in Weybridge, then owned by the Earl of Lincoln, mentions the canal, the menagerie, the greenhouse, the aviary and positively rhapsodises over the 'new Terrace one and a half miles in length' but fails to mention a Grotto. She dismisses the house there as 'not remarkable'.

Amongst other properties Mrs Pye visits Claremont, again belonging to the Pelham family. The house is considered 'an old fashion'd ungraceful building' and in the Park 'there is no Water but what is brought from a distant Spring into a large full Bason, close by the Brink of which is an irregular Rock composed of Spars, Fossils &c, that seems the happy work of nature, such is its elegant Rusticity'. Mrs Pye does not seem to have entered the grotto; if she had done so in 1760 she would probably not have found the internal decoration of minerals and shells that was added by the Lanes of Tisbury according to records held in the National Trust archive. Dating this internal work has to be speculative, but logically it might have followed the end of the initial phase at Painshill, in which case it came before the Lanes' work at Castle Hill, i.e. 1765/6, or just after Castle Hill and before the Lanes recommenced work at Painshill, in which case it would be 1767/8, but the date is unverifiable.

John Parnell, in his Journal dated 1769, recounts that 'There is a Piece of Rockwork at the head of the Piece of water made at Immense Expence and a grotto with 3 chambers communicating by arches. It is very Pretty but I could have a finer Rock with me in half an hour than his grace was able to make there in years and brought all his Rocks by water near as he could to Clermont and thence with waggons, think what an Expence'[3]

Mr Parnell is keen to criticise the 'Expence' lavished upon the grotto but his comment on the method of delivering the rock is interesting – the nearest navigable river was probably the River Wey, although the River Mole runs nearby. The cost of moving stone for any of the grottoes was probably a considerable 'Expence'. It would be interesting to know where it was obtained and how it was moved. Similarly the decorative items such as ammonites, feldspar, etc. had to be obtained and delivered. It was not a negligible expense for the landowner.

In 1769 Robert Clive of India bought Claremont from the Duchess of Newcastle, commissioning 'Capability' Brown to design a new Palladian style mansion on higher ground in place of the old, damp house. He had asthma and sadly died in November 1774, having never slept in his wonderful new mansion. Perhaps he also failed to visit the enhanced interior of his Grotto. Maybe this became a secret place for its subsequent owner's wife, Sarah Delavel, Countess of Tyrconnel who was known to have been the mistress of both the Duke of York and especially the Earl of Strathmore. A wonderful spot in which to conduct a romantic affair, if a bit damp.

Some time later, after the death in childbirth of the heir to the throne, Princess Charlotte, which occurred at Claremont House, the public was admitted to the grounds during the absence abroad of the

Claremont Park, Esher Surrey: the grotto before restoration

The grotto today

grieving widower Prince Leopold. Visitors broke off the stalactites, shells and coral spars, taking them away as souvenirs of the much loved Princess.[4]

By 1975 the grotto had fallen into total disrepair and with silting up from the lake the surrounding area became marshy and inaccessible The sandstone and chalk conglomerate blocks which had replaced the earlier dressed stone cascade had started to deteriorate and fall down so the grotto had to be fenced off from the public. The National Trust reassembled the stones, fixing them together with steel pins, and cleared the marshy ground. A path was created, and a laurel tunnel planted to create the required melancholic atmosphere.[5] It is not known whether the interior was ever restored and this is now totally inaccessible to visitors to Claremont Park.

13

PAINSHILL —

THE CRYSTAL GROTTO COMPLETED

Joseph returned to Painshill in 1768 and this time he took Josiah with him. There was no house there with convenient outbuildings so Joseph and Josiah must have stayed in a village cottage in Cobham, perhaps being looked after by a village widow, who could feed them and do the washing as well. This is supposition, but they stayed at Painshill, working on the interior of the grotto, until 1773. Charles Hamilton had found the necessary capital to continue with his great gardening project, and more imaginative installations had begun.

For the Lanes, the interior at Painshill was detailed, demanding physical and imaginative work. Deliveries of feldspar started to arrive, some colourless and transparent, some coloured or opaque crystals, formed from cooling magma, granite or other igneous rocks. Pink, white, grey and brown crystals, pieces of amethyst from Siberia and Carolina, purple quartz, rose quartz, silver and gold mica flakes. How did Joseph know what he wanted and needed? Huge clam shells and branches of coral from the West Indies, all were duly delivered in their turn and with Josiah fetching and carrying, sorting and splitting, and learning his trade, the Lanes set to work to make Charles Hamilton's grotto one of the wonders of the world, or certainly of England. £8,000 had been allocated for this amazing cavern, and it took the full five years to 1773 to complete.[1]

Now that it has been expertly restored by the late Diana Reynell and by Tessa Hadley under the direction of Cliveden Conservation, the genius of the Lanes can once again be enjoyed.

As the visitor enters down the steps to the passageway, which runs almost level with the little stream, glimpses of water can be seen running under the crystal covered roof of the arch, the crystals reflecting light from the sparkling water and bouncing through the apertures in the tunnel.

The main chamber is dazzling, so highly decorated is it with chips and flakes of crystal. These flakes, again layered by plastering on to inverted cones of wooden lathes to resemble many different sized stalactites, some long, narrow and sharp, some more conical, with many tiny ones in the ceiling. Each are covered in the layers of quartz, spar and bluejohn, calcite or fluorite and there is a patterning of zigzags, reminiscent of Florentine Bargello work, which is a pattern that recurs in the Lanes' future work. It is the imaginative use of reflected light that takes the visitor's breath away. The main opening from the chamber faces west across the lake, catching the late afternoon and early evening sun, light shimmering off the lake and bouncing on the walls, the silvery stalactites and jagged ceiling. Water trickles down walls into side niches, into a giant peach-coloured clam shell, and spills into a pool area adorned with coral spars and seashells. The floor is of crushed shells and sand. The water feeds a fountain in the central pillar, and then collects in a sump, when it returns to the lake, to be repumped into the grotto. In the 18th century these magical water effects had to be managed by the guide who had directed the visitor to the dark tunnel entrance, leaving him to bravely enter the dark unknown. The guide would then dash round the outside of the grotto to the water pump taps, so that by the time the visitor arrived in the main cavern, the water was glittering on the walls, bubbling into the clam shell and pooling in the fountain area.[2] Exiting the heavenly cavern, the stonework of the grotto becomes apparently naturally more rocky and returns the visitor to the more worldly, earthly delights of the rest of the garden.

Further payments were made to Joseph in 1765 and 1766, and another payment of £342 18s.10d. is recorded in 1769, which may well have been for the difficult and time consuming period of the decoration of the grotto. By this date young Josiah, who would have been 13 in 1766,

Painshill: the grotto entrance tunnel, with stream (left); interior chamber (right)

Painshill: interior with giant clam shell

was working with his father, so some of this payment had to cover his earnings too. The final payment to Joseph for Painshill was made as late as May 1772, for the sum of £96 5s. 0d.[3]

Interior looking out towards the lake

In 1773 Charles Hamilton was forced to sell Painshill, but of course the trees went on maturing, the shrubs grew, the follies and the grotto settled in to become part of the landscape. The Duke of Newcastle's friend Horace Walpole did not like the great garden, complaining of the Gothic style used, 'the Goths' he said 'never built summer houses or temples in a garden'.[4] Despite the criticisms from some of his peers, Charles Hamilton's garden came to exemplify all that was successful in the 18th century picturesque style, and now that it is restored, everyone can appreciate his inventive, imaginative garden architecture, his shrub and tree planting, the sloping vineyard, the winding lake, the cedars on the island and of course the glittering, magical, crystal grotto.

14

A DEATH IN SOHO

In June 1770 Alderman Beckford having caught a chill by going out in the rain at Fonthill, rushed back to business in London, where the chill turned to 'a rheumatic fever'. He suffered an unpleasant few days, with violent hiccups and convulsions and at five o'clock on the morning of Thursday 21 June, the Alderman died.[1]

Expressions of grief at his death were numerous and mostly generous. Some of the press praised him as a defender of liberty, a patron of the arts and a good magistrate. But there was speculation as to the cause of his death- was it from something contagious – and a rumour spread that one of his servants had died immediately afterwards of the same complaint. There was also public curiousity about how wealthy he really was, and who would inherit, bearing in mind the Alderman's numerous offspring apart from his legitimate son William. Celebrity fever hit the capital, medals were struck and tankards cast, decorated with flowers and angels surrounding a resemblance of the Mayor. Some people were not so kind, including the waspish Horace Walpole, who commented that 'the papers make one sick'.[2]

The Alderman lay in state for a week at his house in Soho Square, wrapped in his white woollen shroud, allowing time for visitors to peek and commiserate with the widow. On 28 June a simple cortege of three coaches left Town for his last visit to the country. Three coaches, the hearse decorated with plumes and escutcheons, carried the family and the Alderman home to Fonthill. His funeral, on 30 June, was a comparatively simple one; he was buried at the church he had built on the ridge at Fonthill, his coffin carried by six 'country labourers', each of whom had been given a 'gray' suit. Some forty-five of his tenants were in the congregation with his family and his country friends.[3]

No doubt Charles Hamilton was among the mourners and as Joseph and Josiah had been working at Painshill at the time the news had reached Charles, it is likely that they returned home to Tisbury and may well have been two of the six labourers appointed to carry the coffin, since the Lane family had been at Fonthill from the beginning of the Alderman's ownership.

Life expectancy in Georgian England averaged about 35 years – short, although those who managed to survive infancy and early childhood illnesses, might reach late middle age or older, since the estimate includes the huge number of children who died early. But by the middle of the Georgian era living conditions had improved for most people and there were more material comforts available to those who had some money. Prices had dropped so the professional, trade, farming and craftsmen classes could buy more goods in the form of furniture, fabrics, china, glassware and house decorations. Designers like Wedgwood, Chippendale, Sheraton and Hepplewhite became household names. Fewer houses were built from cob and thatch, leading to a reduction in vermin spread diseases, and, especially in towns and cities, houses were built in stone and brick, with slate roofs, since slate could be transported via the canal system from furthest Wales. A two-up, two-down cottage could be bought for £150 upwards, and now building societies were founded, enabling credit worthy citizens to borrow and buy a house.[4]

The country was, by 1770, well into the reign of its third Hanoverian King, George III. The monarch was still directing foreign and religious policies, (and was still staunchly Protestant); he was still in charge of appointing ministers of state, enjoyed huge powers of patronage through the civil list (albeit a rather corrupt system – although perfectly acceptable to everyone as such), and the Whig party still dominated Parliament. Public officials bought their position, which enabled them to benefit from the generous perks and back handers which they received as a normal profit from their office.

Internationally however, there were problems which George III had to face. The newly powerful American colonists resented paying tax without being represented in Parliament and in 1776 rose up and declared Independence for America. The war that followed this Declaration lasted for seven years and cost Britain a great deal of money and loss of prestige and power. By 1783 there were rumblings of great problems in France and in 1789 the French revolted against their leaders and monarch, having the temerity to cut off heads publicly, thus virtually annihilating their own aristocratic class. This caused great trepidation in Britain, for fear the revolt might spread, and as a result the lower classes found themselves and their lives more constrained, and with no power to change things for the better. Discontent grew very gradually however, and would not become a real problem for many years. Caution caused less borrowing availability and speculative builders were amongst those who suffered, some becoming bankrupt. This in its turn meant less work for craftsmen.

A more immediate worry for the poor was the rise in inflation, when land tax went up, sometimes to 20% and therefore rentals rose in turn. Between 1750 and 1790 the cost of renting a home rose by 50% taking up to 20% of the family's income. This bore down heavily in rural areas where families could not afford to buy their own home and were completely dependent upon local richer landowners.[5]

For the middle classes however, life was still pleasant, with the spread of such delights as coffee houses, pleasure gardens like Ranelagh and Vauxhall, spas to visit at Bath, Tunbridge Wells or Cheltenham and a growing awareness that life could offer cultural pleasures too, such as going to look at paintings, or gardens, or even great houses where a letter of introduction enabled visitors to tour the rooms and look at the furniture and decorations. Even the King collected paintings, and was known to have bought £34,000 worth of paintings by Benjamin West.

Many artists were the sons of craftsmen, such as plasterers or stonemasons, these sons becoming the leading artists of the day, some being apprenticed, liked Blake and Hogarth, some simply diversifying from their father's trade. The artist Sir William Opie's father was a carpenter, for example. There seemed to be little distinction in the public mind between being a skilled craftsman and an artist, an architect or a garden designer.

Books were expensive; a novel might cost 7s 6d., a volume of letters or history as much as a guinea. Serials were therefore popular and attainable at 6d a time and the middle classes might be able to join a circulating library.[6]

Much of Georgian cultural life was theatrical and often of a spectacular nature, such as visiting a painted panorama, an open air ball or masque, or watching a bare back riding spectacular such as the ones put on by Philip Astley. Actor-Managers were charge of theatres, putting on dramatic or sentimental plays, operas such as *The Beggars' Opera*, or a visit to a concert might be just what was required. Handel, after composing and presenting many operas to be sung in Italian, had decided that what the English wanted was to understand the words, and so he started writing and producing English based oratorios, confirming to his audience that they were indeed the chosen people, righteous and powerful, his music and the words swelling their hearts with pride. The King too loved Handel's work, going to the theatre to hear his music regularly and setting up the great performances in Westminster Abbey of the *Messiah*, and encouraging presentations of this, the *Music for the Royal Fireworks*, the *Water Music*, and oratorios throughout his kingdom. George III loved music so much he founded the Academy of Ancient Musick, and perhaps music was a comfort to him in the periods of his terrible illness. The composer Arne was popular, and of course Purcell's music was still played. It was a time of appreciation of magnificent, loud and powerful sights and sounds, to stir the heart and strengthen the sinews.

Building a large house which dominated the land was encouraged and some of the most beautiful buildings in Britain were designed and built during this period, architecture setting a standard of elegance and utility which has never been bettered. The habit of sending sons off on the Grand Tour widened appreciation of classical styles so that not only aristocratic families with money could build in the Palladian idiom, but entrepreneurial builders could create whole towns and cities in what has become the much loved Georgian fashion with its elegant, regular terraces, circuses and squares with secluded private communal gardens. In Spa towns the fashionable rich could gather together to enjoy taking the waters for health purposes, to take part in balls and routs, to gamble, to meet a prospective spouse, to see and to be seen. It was important to observe the newly exciting rules of etiquette laid down by a master of ceremonies such as Beau Nash, and to conform to the exacting dress rules laid down by Beau Brummell – the self appointed ring masters of the celebrity society.

Surprisingly, a Protestant work ethic flourished in spite of the rash spending of the new elite. It was felt that happiness was essential but also that work could be an inexhaustible source of pleasurable activity, and without it, health and success could not be achieved. To earn money, to inherit it, and to spend it was perfectly acceptable, and this gave rise to a certain smug self- satisfaction amongst the English, a sense that being English was perhaps the only right and proper way of life and that other religions and nationalities were not quite, shall we say, as deserving of the good life. Of course, one could let in the useful hard working Huguenots and Jews, but everyone must know and accept their allotted place in Society, and this was the only way in which the country could prosper. It was difficult to rid oneself of an innate sense of suspicion against foreigners, or people who were different.

Alderman Beckford then, coming as he did from Jamaica, had achieved a great deal in becoming Mayor of the City of London, a respected and well regarded landowner, a patron of the arts and an MP. How would his son William, who would be one of the richest men in England, make his mark and for the purposes of this book, how would his preferences impact on the lives of Joseph and Josiah Lane?

15

AND ANOTHER IN TISBURY

It is the first day of April in the year of our Lord 1775 and there is a pale, watery sun catching the fragile new leaves in the hedgerows. The banks of the lane are full of cheerful yellow primroses which are quite frankly, Joseph thinks, the only cheerful things to think about at the moment. He simply cannot believe that Deborah's death has happened so suddenly. At Christmas, she had a chill it is true, and a nasty, persistent little cough, but then so did half the village. And it has been a cold wet three months as usual.

Joseph has been trying to comfort both of his daughters, young Deborah and little Rebeckah, and his normally calm and solidly sensible son. News has spread fast as usual in Tisbury and the woman who helps lay out the dead has arrived. His eldest daughter is helping, but Joseph cannot bear to be inside the cottage and has come to sit in the garden to think about his wife. They obviously haven't been able to do much work in the vegetable garden so far this year, although the soil is turned over and the pea and bean sticks await their work of supporting the great green growth of summer. He knows there will be no green growth this year, and getting up, he removes the sticks angrily, bundling them together and stacking them in the shed. It gives him something to do while they lay out the body, dressing her in her best dress for the viewing. He has spoken to the carpenter, who will arrive tomorrow morning with the pine coffin. He will ride down into the village this afternoon to make arrangements with the vicar for the funeral.

Joseph knows that even if Deborah had been able to see a doctor, it is unlikely that any remedy would have been useful and saved his wife. Life expectancy is not much, and a chill turning to bronchitis or pneumonia, a chest infection, or even sometimes an infected wound, can lead quickly to death. Particularly if the patient is under-nourished. I should never have left her alone so much, he thinks, although he knows that Deborah wanted him to succeed and she knew how important his work is to him.

Friends and visitors start to arrive and little Rebeckah has picked some springs of rosemary from the garden, and using black ribbon, has tied little knots to give to each person. Rosemary for remembrance, and practically, it helps to dispel any lingering smells. She thinks her mother looks calm now, no more coughing and struggling for breath as she was when her sister Deborah reached home from Wylye, the village a few miles away where she now lives. She is walking out with a nice young man, Stephen Titt, and is making plans to marry him. Rebeckah realises that her mother won't see any grandchildren now and this moves her to more tears. The girls are glad that they were all together when their mother died, even though it was horrible.

Joseph lights a fire in the living room but the parlour needs to remain cool. When the coffin is delivered, he and Josiah carry Deborah's body carefully downstairs, arrange the white woollen shroud and pillow in the coffin and lay her carefully inside. Her daughters place primroses in her hands. Friends and neighbours arrive, a few at a time, to look at the body, commiserate with the family, and to learn what Joseph and Josiah are doing and where they are working. Many of the men are stonemasons and perhaps a little envious of the unexpected good prospects of these fellow craftsmen.

Joseph saddles up his horse and rides slowly down into Tisbury. He will need to spend quite a bit of money on the funeral, even if it is going to be a simple one. He is thankful that they are not so poor that Deborah's body has to be tipped into a 'poor's hole' – a pit which is left open until filled with the bodies of poor people and only then filled in. He doesn't know if Tisbury has ever had one, but his wife won't have to suffer that. He needs to pay the beadle, the gravedigger, to arrange for the quire and the West Gallery Band with its fiddle player, cello, drum and serpent - he will let them choose the music. Joseph is not a musical man, he doesn't hear much music except in church, and he doesn't go to church often now that he frequently works away from home, but he knows that Deborah enjoys the church band and singing. She will, he thinks, no, she would, he corrects himself, enjoy the music.

The Rev. William Thomas is helpful and kind. Joseph tells him that he, his son, young Stephen Titt and another friend, William Beckett, will carry the coffin, and that they will bring her down on the cart with their own horse. There is no need for black horses, plumes of feathers, pallbearers or any other ceremonial items. This will be a family and friends event. He goes off to the Crown to arrange for beer, bread and cheese for his friends after the service.

Curiously there is quite a cheerful atmosphere in the cottage when he reaches home. His eldest daughter has made a big vegetable stew and baked bread and surprisingly he find he is hungry. Anyway he wouldn't want to upset his daughter by refusing to eat when she has bothered to make a meal. His bed is cold when he reaches it, and lonely without his wife, and although he knows that physically she is still here in the parlour, she is not here at all. He manages to fill in another day by tidying up the garden. Josiah goes out to meet with his friends, and Deborah cleans in the house and welcomes more visitors. Her young man arrives in the evening, and Joseph is pleased to meet him although it is a sad time to welcome him into the family.

The young people go out in the morning to pick more primroses and Rebeckah ties them into little posies. Eventually it is time to leave for church, and the men lift the coffin into the cart. The primrose posies cover the coffin and the little cortege proceeds along Hindon Lane, down the High Street and into Church Street, gathering friends and neighbours as it goes, the church bells, muffled in respect, ringing for Deborah. As they reach the west door the bells cease but the Great bell tolls six times, as is customary for a woman, and the Rev. William Thomas, in his white surplice, greets them. As they enter the church, where Deborah had always worshipped since she came to Tisbury after their marriage, the band starts to play and the quire to sing, a traditional hymn in a suitably minor key. Joseph thinks it is a bit scratchy and has a curiously droning sound, but he knows Deborah would be pleased.

After the simple service, they carry the coffin into the sunny churchyard, where the gravedigger has managed to get a grave dug in good time. Joseph turns aside to put money into the alms box for the poor which is kept in the church porch. His daughters are in tears again, but Josiah is his usual stolid, calm self. People are throwing more flowers into the grave, which would please his wife he thinks. The afternoon sun slants off the cream stones of the big table tombs. He won't be able to afford one of those, but he hopes he can mark her grave in some way – after all he is a stonemason. And all of us will end up here he finally decides. He thanks the vicar and gets his hand shaken in turn.

Off they go to the Crown for beer and food and as is the way after funerals, everyone cheers up and gets quite jolly. He has put more money aside for the quire and the band and they, having brought their instruments, play and sing something much more cheerful. He sits in the window of the Crown, remembering village dances and processions, looking out at the churchyard and wishing she was here to enjoy being with her friends and neighbours.

Afterwards the family returns wearily up the hill, Josiah and Stephen taking turns to walk beside the horse, Joseph and the girls riding in the cart. The fire has gone out in the cottage, only a memory of warmth left in the living room. Soon Joseph and Josiah must leave to start new work at Oatlands Park in Weybridge far away in Surrey. Deborah will go back to Wylye with Stephen where, on the 2nd October of this year, she will marry him. It will be a very simple wedding - she will still be in mourning for her mother, but they will live together in Wylye for a long time and have three children, another Stephen, John and another Deborah. The family decides that Rebeckah should go and live with Deborah and Stephen for the moment, but that they will keep the Tisbury cottage, because although Joseph knows there will be a long period of work at his next job at Oatlands Park, and it looks like years rather than months, the family connection with the village will remain strong.

It's been a very long day. He goes up to his cold bedroom again, and is soon asleep. He dreams of stalactites and ammonites, amethysts, pink shells and flakes of feldspar . . .

16

OATLANDS PARK —
CREATION AND DESTRUCTION

On 20 April 1775 Joseph Lane started work at Oatlands Park, Weybridge, his initial task being to change the exterior of a garden pavilion[1]. This pavilion, built some years earlier and designed by Stephen Wright, [2] (a Surveyor who had been William Kent's assistant and Clerk of the Works at Hampton Court), was to become a grotto, covered in the familiar tufa like pitted limestone, but retaining the formal glazed windows of its upper storey. Oatlands Park was just one of various estates owned by the 9th Earl of Lincoln, who had become 2nd Duke of Newcastle-under-Lyme in 1762. The Duke wished to 'improve' the landscaping of the estate and had employed an army of 'artificers' - bricklayers, masons, carpenters, plumbers, smiths, and plasterers amongst whom was Joseph Lane of Tisbury 'grotto decker' and later, his son Josiah.[3]

The Earl, who was not politically ambitious, but held a number of Government posts including being Auditor of the Exchequer from 1751-

1794, had plenty of time to think about his estates, houses and his dogs. He was responsible for breeding the Clumber spaniel, named after his Nottingham estate, Clumber Park, preferring to spend his time at his estates, pursuing country affairs and gambling. He had asked Lord Burlington to design a Palladian-style villa for Oatlands, which was in existence by 1770, having been sketched that year by a visiting French architect, but visitors to Oatlands fail to mention it, with the exception of the redoubtable Mrs Henrietta Pye, who dismisses it as 'unremarkable'. However, she does refer to various other buildings, and there were some delightful pavilions such as the 'pretty building' designed by William Kent on the Terrace, two Doric pavilions, a Temple of Venus by Stephen Wright and a Temple of Vesta. All these, and the original grotto pavilion were erected between 1740 and 1775, the grotto being designed by Stephen Wright, now Oatlands Estate Manager, and assembled under his direction.

The Newcastle archive collection holds the accounts provided by Stephen Wright between 1775 and 1778 which directly relate to the redesigning of the grotto and the building of the hothouse amongst other items. Maybe Joseph had already started work there in 1774 but his invoices start for the year of 1775, the first one referring to his 'work at the grotto' from 20 April to 14 November 1775, being 20 weeks and four days at two and half guineas per week - £75 5s 0d. This account was paid by Stephen Wright on the 13th November of that year, minus the ten guineas already advanced to Joseph that summer. By 28 April Joseph had installed himself at the house of Mr. Jonas Brown in Weybridge, his lodging cost there being the sum of 1s per week, a total of £1 8s.0d. for 28 weeks to 17 November. This seems to have been for Joseph only, because Josiah is not mentioned at all in the 1775 accounts. Perhaps he stayed in Tisbury that year, or perhaps he is simply not mentioned in his father's invoice.[4]

Much of the early work on renovating the grotto was to naturalise the exterior so that it looked more like a cave below the upper structure which was to remain a formal pavilion with windows. It would overlook a pond or small lake, with its lower storey faced in the pitted, knobbly limestone. Some stone was delivered by barge from London to Walton by a Mr J Taylor, Bargeman, at a cost of £16 and lead sheeting also arrived. By July James Edgell the glazier was cleaning and reputtying the glazing of the windows and painting the woodwork. Some of the most interesting invoices are those submitted by the smiths, Mr Keene and later Mr Sershall, for all the tool maintenance, chisel sharpening, hammer steeling and replacement, mattock repair, making cramps of various sizes, hooks, nails, nuts and screws, bolts and plates. Every year these smiths submitted detailed invoices for the repair and maintenance of all the items used in construction – this was continuous work and without it, Joseph could not have created the incredible interior of the grotto or do the heavy outside work.

At the end of November the work stopped - and everyone was paid for the year. This meant that all the 'artificers' had to learn to manage their incomes sensibly. No doubt there was a lot for the Lanes to do in the cottage and garden in Tisbury, and Christmas could be spent in the company of the family at Wylye.

In 1776 Joseph returned to Weybridge and this time Josiah was definitely with him, as the invoice to Stephen Wright for that year covers the 37 weeks' work from 9 April to 24 December, for 'self and son' at three guineas per week, a total of £116 11s.0d. In addition he submits a charge for 15 weeks' board for self and son at 8s. each (£1) and 22 weeks' lodging at 2s. per week (£2 4s. 0d.) He receives on account the sum of £18 8s 0d. early in the year and so collects £112 7s. 0d., but he does not actually receive this until 7 July 1777, so has had to make his previous year's income, and his advance of £18 8s. 0d. last some considerable time.[5] However, with the average weekly wage of a labourer now averaging less than 10s. per week, Joseph probably considers his income to be adequate, with their board and lodging paid for, plus three guineas a week for nine months of the year, giving him and Josiah each more

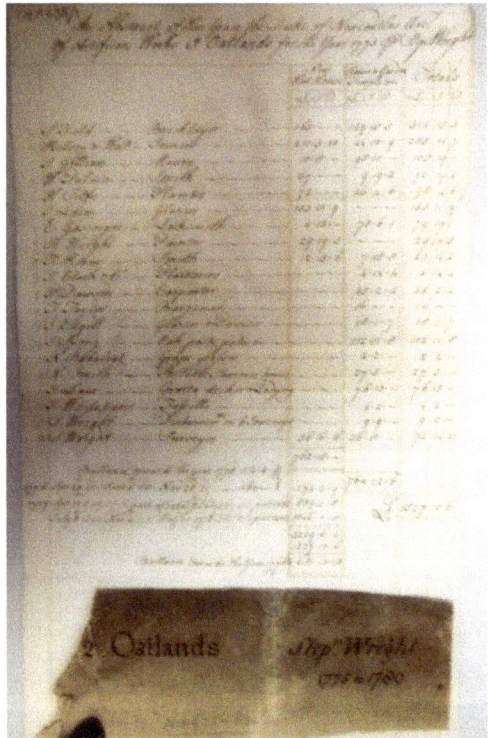

Stephen Wright's Abstract of costs for Oatlands Park grotto, Weybridge Surrey

than double the average weekly income. It must have been at about this time that Joseph began to think of buying another cottage and a little land in Fonthill Gifford.

It is revealing to compare the money that the Duke of Newcastle was prepared to pay his highly regarded 'grotto decker' Joseph Lane for the newly renovated grotto, with the earnings of other artists/craftsmen of the period, such as the Italian stuccatori, or decorative plasterers, who were so busy at this time working on the ceilings and walls of newly built Georgian mansions. The cost of a stucco ceiling by one of these craftsmen varied from £35 for a small, modestly decorated dressing room for example, to over £500 for a magnificent, figuratively decorated saloon ceiling, with swags, fruit flowers and putti. These stuccatori were trained in the arts of drawing and modelling, working their way upwards through unpaid apprenticeships, to journeyman, master and eventually working principal. They worked in workshop teams, travelling all over Europe, the principal negotiating the contracts, usually for a 36-week season, and sometimes for many seasons in one place over a number of years, providing all their own equipment and assistants' wages. A working principal would be paid by bank draft rather than cash, and although lower down in the prestige scale than an artist/painter, he would be considered to be someone of some status amongst the peripatetic builders of the period. In 1754 two of the best known stuccatori, the Lafranchini brothers from northern Italy, were paid £910 by the Duke of Northumberland for two seasons' work on Northumberland House, by seven separate bank drafts drawn on Hoare's Bank. This works out at six guineas per week for each of the brothers, who would have had to pay out of this their materials, scaffolding and working journeymens' wages.[6] Joseph's three guineas a week for a 37 week season only 23 years later, shows him to be a highly valued artist/craftsman.

In 1776 the work on the interior really starts, with bricklayers, carpenters and Mr Selfe the plumber involved. A delivery of 30 tons of 'pick'd Grotto stuff at 5s. per ton' arrives from Robert Vigne & Co., a glass manufactory in Southwark 'the 12 baskets' in which it is packed to be returned. From Eleanor Coade, decorative Coade stonework and artificial stone capitals are ordered at a cost of £307 3s.6d. although these may have been destined for a different garden works.[7]

The completed grotto was a substantial building, with three rooms on the lower floor and a large, liveable, decorated upper chamber reached by ramps. It had a core of red brick, now covered in the tufa

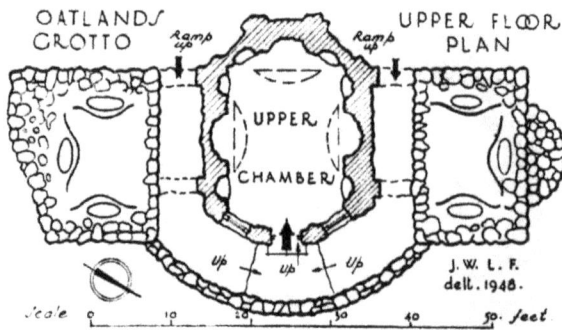

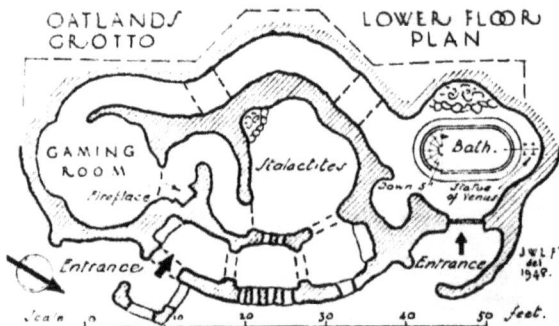

Grotto floor plans by J W Lindus Forge ARIBA

like limestone, with a string course of dressed stone, giant ammonites and 'brain coral', with porthole windows decorating the lower part of the grotto. Inside the lower part which could be accessed from entrances at either end linked by a curving, arched passage with an opening giving a view out onto the little lake, lay three separate rooms. The little lake was fed by a pipe conducting water from nearby St George's Hill and contained goldfish. The acerbic Mr Horace Walpole once again acting as a downbeat Greek chorus, termed this 'a basin of dirty water'. Later the conduit was cut by the construction in 1838 of the London to Southampton railway and the little lake had to be replaced with a wooded copse.

The ceilings of the passage-way were covered in patterns created by selenite, red calcite and vitreous blue material. At the end of the passage an arch led into the central chamber, by all accounts the most amazing, dazzling, mystical place. Its ceiling was densely covered in Joseph's trade-mark stalactites of different lengths, grouped au naturel and covered in glistening spar. The two concealed yeux de boeuf gave just enough light to catch the glistening glass, but gave the visitor a sense of shadowy, mysterious spaces extending away from him into dark corners. Another arched entrance then led through a further narrow, winding passage into the next chamber, known as the Gaming Room, which was supplied with a fireplace complete with firedogs and grate. The gaming den was no doubt the place of much enjoyment for the Duke and his friends. He was apparently a good host, a gambler and teller of bawdy tales and the 'den' was supplied with comfortable cushions worked by the Duchess' own hand. There is no record of her opinion on the bawdy stories. Lolling on the cushions, the well- bred friends could gaze in wonder at the star and zigzag patterns of the roof decorations, which after a few glasses of madeira may have seemed quite strange and disorientating.[8]

The third chamber in the lower grotto was entered by yet another narrow corridor leading from the gaming room, curving around the back of the grotto, to a room with an enormous bath, ten feet nine inches long, five foot wide and five foot deep, filled with freezing cold water. The walls were lined with small shells set inside out into the plaster, and with the occasional giant cowrie shell. Here stood a copy of the 2nd century Venus de Medici. The bath no doubt cooled down the over-stimulated gamblers who could leave this chamber through a door to the lakeside.

Oatlands: the central chamber photographed in 1937 (left); interior of the upper room, drawn by Barbara Jones in 1940 (right)

In 1777 Joseph and Josiah worked at Oatlands from 15 April until 11 November, earning £93 9s. 0d. for 30 weeks' work by Joseph and 20 by Josiah. Board and lodging came to £9 18s. 0d. and the advance that year was six guineas. On 6 November Joseph and Josiah were paid the balance owing of £97 1s. 0d.

Work at the grotto had continued during that year with four large loads of large flintstones being delivered, for which Josiah was authorised to hand over £1 6s. 0d to the provider, John May. Richard Horley picked and delivered three loads of flints for the grotto at 6s. per load (£1 4s. 0d.) and the cost of providing two men for one day at 3s. One lot of old stones from the old Somerset House arrived, with sundry pieces of ornament £5 5s. 0d. from Sir William Chambers (who was probably building the new Somerset House at the time). Mr Thomas Keene the smith, submitted his account for tool repairs and replacements in the sum of £6 9s. 0d. for no less than 52 separate occasions.[9]

Now work could proceed on the upper chamber. This beautiful room was reached by two ramps and a few steps up, each ramp extraordinarily decorated with horses' teeth and pigs' trotter bones. The ramps inspired Horace Walpole to comment 'and which never happened to a grotto before, . . . lives up one pair of stairs'. One can only assume that Walpole was considered to be witty, but he seems to be consumed with envy for other people's grottoes.[10]

The upper room measured 22'9" by 18' and was much used and loved by the family. Henry Bushell was the painter who was responsible for the doors and woodwork of the windows. In 1777 he stayed at Oatlands, charging 3s. for the three weeks' lodging and 12s. for travelling costs. He provided paint in delicious colours – Naples Yellow, Burnt Umber, Terra di Sienna, Prussian Blue, Fine Lake and Vermillion. The plasterers had mixed the boiled oil and turpentine for the plaster flooring, colouring the mix with red lead, white lead and lamp black.[11]

Only a couple of months' work was left for Joseph and Josiah in 1778, from 17 March to 23 June, when they worked for 14 weeks at three guineas a week for 'self and son' £44 2s. 0d. and board and lodging for ten weeks cost another eight guineas. The advance at the beginning of that year was two guineas and Joseph then received the balance of £50 8s. 0d. on 23 June 1778. It is interesting to note that each account, although written in Stephen Wright's elegant hand, is signed by 'me Joseph Lane', his signature exactly as it is in the Letters of Administration of 1748.[12]

In the upper room the large gothic style windows looked out over the lake and the great canal, which apparently stretched into the distance, although this was achieved by clever planting – the distant water was in fact the River Wey. Candelabras hung from the stalactite encrusted ceiling, and the candle flames were reflected in great mirrors hung from coral branches, creating a magical glittering space. Heraldic glass panels in the windows were coloured cobalt blue, red and gold and a frieze of quartz, stalactites and pink and white shells edged the lower walls. Chinese

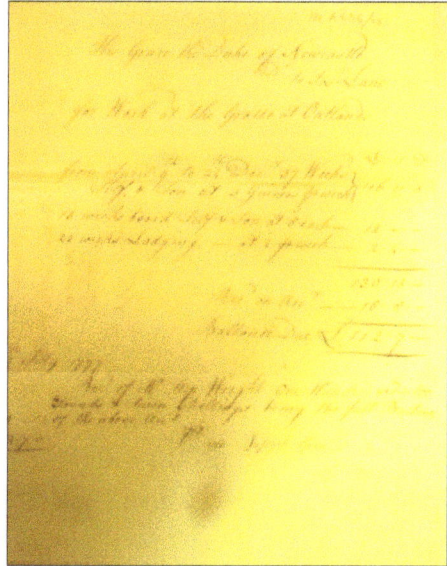

Joseph Lane's receipted invoice for grotto work at Oatlands

Chippendale style bamboo chairs with embroidered cushions provided a comfortable place to sit and enjoy the sunshine which streamed in through the big windows.

In 1788 our old friend Horace Walpole paid a visit to this masterpiece and although he was keen to see it, he was, as usual, less than kind – commenting in a letter to the Countess of Ossory on the 9th July; [13]

> Thursday. Woe is me! I don't know whether it is that I am grown old and cross, but I have been disappointed. Oatlands, that my memory had taken into its head as the centre of Paradise, is not half so Elysian as I used to think.

Later, when Oatlands became the property of the Duke and Duchess of York, the Duchess kept twenty dogs, parrots and horses, although the latter were not for riding. She enjoyed playing with her pets and they ended up in a little cemetery just below the grotto.

In November 1791 the composer Joseph Haydn came to stay with the Duke and Duchess, playing for them for four hours each evening.[14] His comments are kinder than Mr Walpole's –

The little castle 18 miles from London, lies on a slope and
commands the most glorious view. Amongst its many beauties is
a most remarkable grotto which cost £25,000 sterling, and which
was eleven years in the building. It is very large and contains
many diversions, inter alia actual water that flows in from various
sides, a beautiful English garden, various entrances and exits,
besides a most charming bath.

It is nice to imagine Mr Haydn making music in the upper
chamber, lit by a myriad candle flames, the sound bouncing off the
glittering ceiling and walls, the select audience dressed in shiny silks
and satins.

The creation of the grottoes at Oatlands, and Painshill, together
with the forthcoming work at Ascot Place, puts the Lanes, in the opinion
of garden historian Barbara Jones, 'among the greatest artists of the 18th
century'.[15]

In 1815 the upper room was the venue for a post Battle of Waterloo
supper, when the Emperor of Russia and three other kings were
present.[16] The gold and silver on the dining table, the white and gold
and red sashes of the uniforms, the flowers and fruit all had to compete
with the glitter of the white spar, pink and white shells, the huge mirrors
reflecting the little flames of the wall candles held by coral sconces, and
the shine and sparkle of the silvery stalactites.

In its later years the Grotto was well cared for by various owners,
until the Second World War, when Oatlands was occupied by our own
troops; the fences around the garden went unrepaired and soldiers used
the grotto windows as target practice, and no doubt used the grotto for
various other activities. By the end of the War it looked as though it had
been the object of enemy action and the then owners of Oatlands Park,
North Hotels, decided it should be demolished, rather than more money
having to be spent on repairing it. They applied to Weybridge Urban
District Council for a licence to demolish, on the grounds that it was
'unsafe'. The UDC 'forgot' an undertaking that Surrey County Council
must be informed before any decision could be taken, and although
both the Georgian Group and caring local residents tried to stop the
destruction, and questions were asked in Parliament, permission was
apparently granted by the UDC. Hansard records that the Minister of
Town & Country Planning, Mr Silkin, replying to a question by Mr
Keeling MP on 17 February 1948 said that the licence to demolish was

in fact issued by the Ministry of Works in view of representations by the Surveyor to the UDC that the building was dangerous and that Surrey CC learned too late to stop the destruction. The minister commented that 'he was very sorry' about it.[17]

Fortunately a complete record was made in the few weeks left before demolition, measured drawings were prepared by Mr J. W. Lindus Forge ARIBA, photographs were taken by Mr Cookson of the University of London Archaeological Department and, luckily, Barbara Jones had already drawn a delightful sketch of the upper room. Demolishing the grotto was harder work than expected, but eventually it fell victim to the picks and shovels of the demolition men. Pneumatic drills had to be used to destroy the stone and brickwork and today nothing is visible in the hotel grounds. Apparently a few stalactites, shells and an iron window were taken to Weybridge Museum and the Medici Venus also resided there. The Duchess of York's small cemetery for her pets had been restored during the Victorian period at the request of the Queen. Now the little tombstones were moved and can still be seen close to the hotel. The great landscape garden with its canal and magnificent terrace is still somewhere to walk and enjoy the trees and the views, but none of the picturesque garden buildings survive.

The writer Denton Welch (1915–1948) visited Oatlands with his father during the thirties. For a boy of fifteen he was unusually aware of how delightful the Grotto must have been, writing about it in his book *In Youth is Pleasure* in 1958. His vivid prose is reminiscent of the younger William Beckford's nearly two hundred years earlier. Welch here describes his hero's visit to the Grotto:

> He turned the heavy ring, and, as before, the door opened easily. The same smell of slime and bats' dung and earth met him. He lashed the light upwards immediately, afraid of the bats.
>
> What he saw amazed him. All the walls of the cave were filled with giant shells, feldspars, quartzes, stalactites and fossils. In one place, a thin trickle of water dripped from pink lip to pink lip of beautiful and enormous scallop-shells. In the centre of the cave stood a monumental stone table and stools carved like dolphins with their tails in the air. King George IV had once been entertained to dinner here by the son of the duke who made the grotto, but Orvil knew nothing of this. He loved the grotto for itself alone as something beautiful and strange.

His visits to Oatlands obviously had a profound effect upon Welch. In 1948 he heard about the destruction of the Grotto and records in his Journal on the 28th May : [18]

> They have destroyed the Grotto at Oatlands, the one that I wrote about in *In Youth is Pleasure*.
>
> When I was with my father at Oatlands in the nineteen-thirties, how I would love to wander down in the wickedly neglected, enchanted little corner!
>
> Destruction is much more than a negative power. It is an evil force at work every moment. It is just another form of cruelty. The Grotto was condemned as 'dangerous'. The Architectural Review says the great brick piers underneath, the stones, the stalagmites, the shells and other lovely nonsense, were utterly strong for much more than another hundred years. It was only some of the ornamentation which was loose. This is exactly what I remember as a child of fifteen. The whole place was left to fall to pieces, but only a few fragments lay about mournfully on the floor covered with its dead leaves and other garden rubbish. Surely a little cement and good repairing costs less than destroying the whole place with pneumatic drills?
>
> When something beautiful and fantastic that will never be made again is destroyed, one feels that the earth is just that bit drearier, less previous, more worthy of its Surveyor and Urban District Councils.
>
> How wonderful it must be to be on the side of the destroyers! Almost everything sooner or later would fall into your lap.

As a few last words on the destruction of the grotto at Oatlands, a lost Lane masterpiece, his comments can hardly be improved.

17

WIMBLEDON HOUSE, JOSEPH'S DEATH
AND BACK TO FONTHILL

The last years of Joseph's life were partly spent at home in Tisbury but there was one last project for which he is likely to have been responsible, the cascade and grotto at Wimbledon House in Surrey, which was started in 1778, work continuing there until at least 1783. This would have been the work of both Joseph and Josiah. However, nothing is really known about how this grotto looked, as it has now completely disappeared and in only one drawing is it even slightly visible. The grotto does appear quite clearly marked on a plan of Wimbledon House garden, which appeared in Loudon's *Suburban Gardener and Villa Companion* dated 1838 and Loudon also provides a 'View from the Grotto', though sadly not the exterior or interior, and no view of the cascade either.[1]

The house and grounds of Wimbledon House were at that time in the possession of Mr Benjamin Bond Hopkins, a Turkey merchant of Broad Street in the City, who bought it in 1777, having also become the new owner of Painshill earlier in 1773. Mr Bond Hopkins had inherited some £300,000 from a relative on his mother's side, a gentleman known as 'Vulture' Hopkins, who had amassed his great fortune by becoming a usurer, and was well known as a miser and notorious for his rapacity.

Whether the 'Turkey' in Benjamin's career description relates in any way to the 'Vulture' in his relative's nickname is an interesting question. Both are large noisy birds, but the turkey is somewhat less unpleasant. In fact Benjamin would have traded with Turkey, as a member of the Levant Company. He became an MP, first for Ilchester, and then for Malmesbury. He certainly had sufficient resources to indulge himself in buying both Painshill from Charles Hamilton, who went to live in Bath, and Wimbledon House.

With regard to the grotto at Wimbledon, it seems logical to conclude that since Benjamin had a marvellous grotto at Painshill, he would also need new one at his new residence in Wimbledon. He would therefore have been pleased to employ Joseph and Josiah to provide this little luxury.

Loudon, the garden journalist however, writing about the 'cascade and grotto' in 1838, although mentioning that the 'rockworks' at 'Painshill, Oatlands and Wimbledon House were put up by a stonemason who devoted himself entirely to this kind of production, and who was eagerly sought for in every part of the country' having 'a natural genius for this kind of work' unfortunately then went on to attribute the cascade and grotto at Wimbledon to Bushell, although two years before this Loudon had attributed Oatlands Park grotto quite correctly, to Joseph Lane.[2] He may have been thinking of Thomas Bushell's work at Enstone in Oxfordshire, although this was much earlier, as Bushell lived in the 17th century. This unfortunate attribution was accepted at the time as fact, and other writers in the Victorian period continued to assert that Bushell was the grotto builder at Wimbledon.

Wimbledon House grotto and cascade, if there was a cascade, disappears from even the estate surveys by 1911, the house being knocked down in 1900 and the estate sold for suburban house building. The last mention of a grotto is in an Abstract of Title of the Estate in 1901, which refers to a 'Grotto Field[3]'.

Between 1781 and 1784, William Beckford was creating his Alpine Gardens at Fonthill, planting oaks, beech, elm and fir trees, providing green walks edged with shrubs. Rocks were left in situ to provide a sense of alpine scenery. At this time he changed the lake considerably, enlarging the river bed, demolishing the old Palladian bridge and forming a new dam and cascade at the newly widened southern end of the lake.[4] Although the stretch of water now resembled a lake, it was and still is, a river flowing from north to south, rejoining the Fonthill Brook on its way to Tisbury, where it joins the River Nadder. The water in the lake was drained in 1783 to enable the new work to be completed.

If Joseph and Josiah worked on this new expanded watery scheme, it was the last work they did together, as in 1784 Joseph died and on 28 July he was buried, presumably beside his wife Deborah and their little dead babies, in the churchyard of St John the Baptist in Tisbury.[5] No record of the grave is now available – no doubt reorganisation of the churchyard taking place from time to time, some headstones are moved – many are stacked to one side of the churchyard for example. The church records do not have the Lanes listed amongst the visible table and sleeper tombs or headstones, but as the site has been the burial ground for Tisbury residents for some eight hundred years, this is hardly surprising. There are so many bodies buried there that it would be impossible if everyone had a headstone.

How Joseph died is another unknown. He was 67 at the time of his death, had obviously been a very strong man, but he had worked hard both physically and mentally, travelling a great deal for work in difficult times to travel, and he had become through his own efforts and some luck, one of the country's greatest designers, albeit in a small field. He must have been an intelligent, thoughtful, knowledgeable and enterprising man to have achieved so much and to be so much

Joseph Lane's Will, July 1784

in demand. He could write, he could certainly interpret plans and drawings, he understood the plumbing and engineering necessary to create water flows, he could assess quantities and qualities of materials, arrange to order them, and use them economically. He trained his son Josiah to take over the business and to keep up his contacts.

By the second week of July 1784 Joseph must have known he was very ill and close to death because he decided to make a Will. On 16 July he manages to sign it in front of two witnesses, William Beckett and James Moore. His signature is a little shaky but written nearly as clearly as it is on the signed receipts for his wages from Stephen Wright six years earlier. In his Will he leaves £100 to each of his daughters, and his estate called Jerrards to his youngest daughter Rebecca [*sic*]. This property is at the northern end of Fonthill Gifford, a substantial cottage

Jerrards, Fonthill Gifford in 2017

with adjacent barns and a small amount of land. There is no mention of a property in Wylye, where Deborah lives with her husband Stephen Titt, although this property is, by 1798, in the ownership of Josiah, with Stephen as his tenant. Perhaps the property had been bought specifically for Deborah, but kept in the ownership of her brother.

Josiah receives Joseph's estate called Dowdings, with the Cyder Mill, and Press and Mash Tubb (obviously a very important asset). In addition he receives one third of Joseph's remaining estate, the other two-thirds being shared between Deborah and Rebeckah. Josiah is also appointed sole Executor and given the right to buy the other shares at a proper valuation.

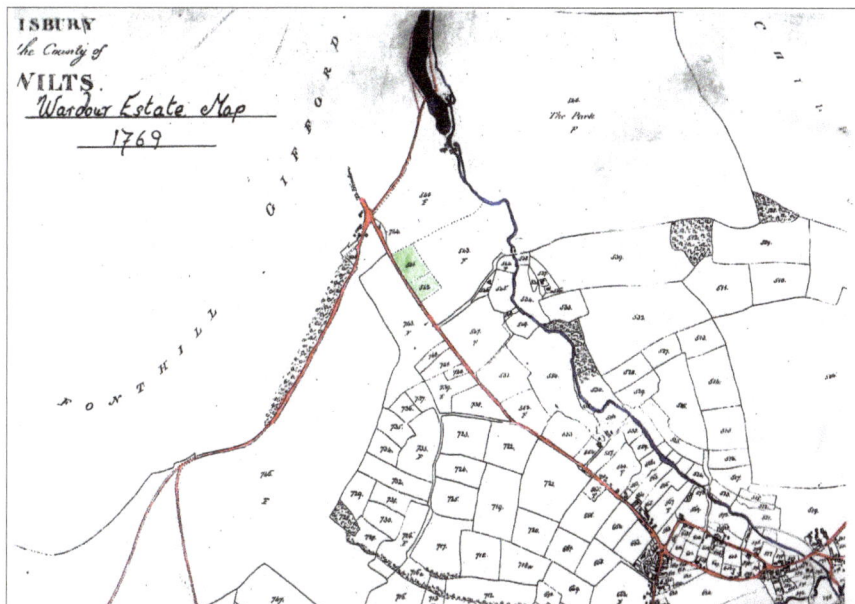

Wardour Estate Map 1769, showing the land known as Dowdings

The Will is proved at Sarum on 15 September 1784 before Edward Moore, Surrogate for the Archdeacon, before the Registrar William Boucher.[6]

So Joseph had managed to become financially successful, i.e. in retaining and using his earnings for the benefit of the family. Certainly father and son were paid well from Painshill, Oatlands and probably Wimbledon, so it is hardly surprising that Joseph managed to buy at least two properties, and possibly three, making a good provision for his family. It was now up to Josiah to continue with the building of the grottoes, but for the time being he was probably on his own in the cottage in Tisbury, then known as Dowdings. Rebeckah had her own home at Jerrards and on 29 November 1786 she married Stephen Spencer, in Tisbury.[7]

Josiah was now aged 31. The work at Wimbledon had ended and although there was always work available to a stonemason of his ability, at Fonthill for example, it is surprising to find that grotto building was recommenced there at that time, as this was a period of great upheaval for young newly married William Beckford, whose mind was certainly on other, more personal, matters. Josiah was, as yet, unmarried, but perhaps now thinking that it was time he too found a partner..

Josiah could be found working again at Fonthill during 1784, when young William Beckford returned from one of his long absences abroad. This trip had been undertaken with Beckford's new wife Lady Margaret Gordon, who he had married in 1783 following a journey to Italy during which William had fallen out with his travelling companion, John Robert Cozens, a watercolourist; William fell ill, his musician John Burton had died of the fever caught from his employer, and Lady Hamilton, William's confidante, had finally succumbed to her long decline from tuberculosis. So the marriage, the family hoped, would help to improve William's spirits and his standing in society, which had always been rather suspect. This trip had been to Paris and Geneva. In Paris William managed to attend a Masonic ritual in an underground temple, and in Geneva Lady Margaret suffered her first miscarriage. By May 1784 the young couple were back in Fonthill.

Throughout that summer Beckford was conducting a correspondence with Dr Samuel Henley, trying to persuade his friend to visit Fonthill to view his new creation of 'rocks and water, which is wonderfully expanded' and in October of the year he writes to Henley that 'Mr Lane is rockifying, not on the high places, but in a snug copse by the riverside . . .' [8] This does seem to refer to the grotto complex on the eastern side of the lake, where by this time the beech and larch trees were more mature, hiding the old scar of the quarry workings. The site now lent itself to a much more romantic spot for walks and contemplation. Beckford was very involved at the time in his thoughts for his new novel *Vathek*, and wanted to create an Alpine garden with the secluded bathhouse and grotto, a series of tunnels leading in and out of an inner temple like cavern, perhaps based on his architect and masonic friend Ledoux' Parisian temple and plans for the 'City of Chaux'. All this was inspired by the idea of a spiritual journey in Beckford's mind, a passing from the neo-Palladian world of Fonthill Splendens to a pagan, mystical world on the other side of the lake, a world which flourished in Beckford's fertile imagination.

The grottoes on which Josiah was working in 1784 are natural and rough in their exteriors, heavier and more Neolithic. However, since Josiah was to start work at Bowood the following year, it seems unlikely that the grottoes were entirely built by him in 1784 and more likely that he was reworking the originals to suit the designs envisaged by his employer, by 'rockifying' the exteriors to appear more savagely picturesque, and maybe adding to the group since Beckford refers to 'wonderfully expanded'.

Fonthilll: the lower, lakeside grotto

Fonthill: the entrance to the lakeside grotto

Since Josiah was installing very large, heavy stones, he would certainly have needed additional physical help now that he no long had his father with him, and perhaps this is where the connection with the older John Burton occurs, then still a young and probably strong man. By 1798 Mr Burton would become the tenant of one of the family homes, possibly the cottage then known as Dowdings.[9]

The stones for these grottoes would have been cut from the old Fonthill Quarry above the eastern side of the lake, and moved downhill to the grotto site. Inside too, the roofs are less elaborately decorated, the jagged spikes not really like stalactites but of a more natural rocky appearance, contrasting with the cut stones of the bath. The rocks are carefully but not artistically assembled, and appear more thrillingly dark and mysterious. The patterns have gone, to be replaced by huge,

Interior of that grotto   The upper, bath-house grotto at Fonthill

seemingly accidental, realistic assemblies of rocks and crystals. A major change in the Lane style has occurred. It is less a delightful place for drinks and dalliance, now a place much more likely to create a frisson of fear in the visitor, the freezing water supplying the bath trickling down through channels to the lower grotto, and into the lake, the damp mosses and snakelike young ferns combining to create a chilling experience. Candlelight would create threatening shadows and the dark, narrow winding passageways lead to low arched exits. What a relief to reach the

sunlight of the delightful terraced walk and to see the shining waters
of the lake. All very Gothick and mysterious. Just what young Beckford
liked and Josiah was happy to oblige. He had known William all his life
and while their life experiences were incredibly different, Josiah was
glad to be working at Fonthill in familiar surroundings in which he felt
at home, and where his father and grandfather had worked. Still, it was
a sad year for him, and perhaps these feelings of loss and sadness are
suggested in the Fonthill grottoes.

There is a delightful description written in July 1791 by Baron
Johan van Biljoen, of work in progress at Fonthill[10]

> . . . There are also some artificial grottoes, a particularly fine
> one with a cold bath and another where the water seeping from
> the top was forming stalactites. Men were occupied in levelling
> the irregularities of a hill so that the slope was swarming with a
> quantity of workmen, who, taken together with a flock of some
> 200 or 300 sheep, greatly animated a landscape already very
> picturesque in itself.

Josiah and John Burton may have worked on through the usual
cold wet Wiltshire winter to complete William's fantasy world for him,
because by July of 1785, William had gone again. Lady Margaret had
suffered another lost baby, this time a son, in May of 1784, and was
once again pregnant when in October, the couple were invited to stay at
Powderham Castle. This was the home of William's young love, William
Courtenay. Beckford, succumbing to temptation, once again dallied with

the boy. This was discovered and accusations of sodomy were published in the papers, so although his young wife stood by him, probably because she had known all along about William's dual sexuality, and chose to ignore it, and she was about to be delivered of their first daughter, it became necessary for them to tactfully retreat to the Continent once again, until the drama had settled. So in July, after the birth of their daughter in April, the family set off for Geneva.[11]

It was fortunate for Josiah then, that his next large contract came along at this moment, the cascade and grotto at Bowood Park in northern Wiltshire, for the 1st Marquis of Lansdowne.

18

WILD WATERFALLS –

JOSIAH AT BOWOOD PARK

Josiah was contacted for his next project through the Hon. Charles Hamilton, for whom he and his father had worked at Painshill. Since then Charles' fortunes had declined, he having lost his lucrative posts of Clerk to the Household of Frederick Prince of Wales, and Receiver-General of the revenues of Minorca, the island which Britain lost to the French in 1756. Through his friend Henry Fox he was in receipt of a secret service pension of £1,200 p.a but this was not enough to prevent a compulsory sale of his beloved Painshill to Benjamin Bond Hopkins in 1773.

Charles retired to Bath, where he bought no. 14 Royal Crescent, which was newly built, and benefitted from a long sloping garden where he could grow rare plants and continue his interest in viticulture. Whether he made wine from his Bath vines is not known. Charles was much in demand by his friends for landscaping and gardening advice. One of his last and finest ideas was for a cascade and grotto at Bowood Park in north Wiltshire for his friend the 1st Marquess of Lansdowne, formerly mentioned here as William 3rd Earl of Shelburne, for whom

Joseph had built the cascade at Loakes Manor in West Wycombe. William had now inherited Bowood and was concentrating on landscaping the grounds.

The plans for a water course were drawn up by Hamilton in 1781, and reflected the changing tastes for a wilder, more natural looking, less decorated landscape. The design was based upon the painting by Poussin of the Tivoli falls.[1] However, what Josiah eventually built in 1785 was a magnificent pile of stones down which cascaded, for thirty feet, the overflow from Capability Brown's winding lake. To the sides and rear of the great boulders Josiah built grottoes and tunnels, through which the visitor could see by means of apertures, the sheets of falling water. Down the stones the water splashed, ending in a stream meandering through a natural looking rocky valley. It was twice the size of the Loakes Manor cascade and much more complicated. This gave rise to a comment by Lord Lansdowne in 1785:[2] 'Lane is much improved in his rockwork which is much advanced and will certainly be finished against Winter'.

Whether this refers to an improvement in the rockwork since the work began that year, as Josiah enlarged and improved on Charles Hamilton's original plan, or whether Lord Lansdowne is comparing it with the work done by Joseph at Loakes Manor twenty-three years earlier, is not known. Josiah would have been only nine years old at the time of the Loakes Manor work, but he may have been with his father, even if only on a fetching and carrying small items basis. At that age he would have been more of a hindrance than a help, but he may have been reminded of himself when, it is said, Henry, the small boy who became the 3rd Marquess, fell down the partly completed cascade at Bowood. The usually solitary and apparently taciturn Josiah would have had to rush to rescue him and dust him down, but luckily Mr Cross, a workman or steward at Bowood, picked him up.[3] He was, it is reported, 'only a little bruised'. Josiah has been rather unfairly called taciturn, but perhaps working mostly on his own, and moving stones with his own hands, made him a silent, thoughtful man. He was also described in later life as 'perfectly ignorant' which now seems unkind, but perhaps people thought of him as a simple man, in a complimentary way. He was certainly a perfectionist in his work, like his father.

Josiah also built a small hermit's cave at the end of the lake, with jagged stones around the mouth of the grotto, using ammonites in the ceiling and walls, where the visitor could sit and gaze upon the Capability Brown lake and the distant view of the house.

Bowood Park: the ceiling of the lakeside Hermitage, with ammonites

Bowood: the exterior of the Hermitage

These fossils could have come from the Chilmark or Tisbury area, which is rich in ammonites. Stonemasons working in the area had long been aware that many fossils could be found in the limestone beds of the Tisbury and Chilmark areas, including the spiral shapes of what came to be called ammonites. These were named for the rams' horns of the Egyptian God Ammon, but it seems unlikely that these craftsmen or workers had any idea why the ammonites were there, or what they were. They were used decoratively locally, appearing in the walls of the stone cottages of the 17th and 18th centuries. Joseph and Josiah naturally found them an attractive way to decorate grottoes, using them to adorn ceilings or form floors and to pattern walls. It is not until the early 19th century that the study of fossils by scientists revealed and classified these beautiful objects as remains from a world hundreds of millions of years before, and conclude that they had been living organisms. By 1830 Henry de la Beche was able to paint an imaginative watercolour of 'A More ancient Dorset' based upon the fossils found by Mary Anning along the Jurassic beaches and cliffs of her native Dorset. At last, the ammonite could take its place as part of the living history of the limestone regions. Jeremy Bentham spent some time at Bowood and at the end of August 1781, wrote to his father requesting a parcel of the most 'shewy' fossils from the Isle of Sheppey, as Bentham wished to give them to his friend Lord Shelburne as a gift.[4] These would not, however, have been the ammonites used in the roof of the hermit's cave grotto, as the fossils from the Sheppey beds are from a different period.

A considerable amount of work went into the cascade, starting in 1785 with the substructure and the laying out of the water course. This was done by a firm of masons from Bath, Messrs. William Reeves. On 9 September of that year Josiah received three guineas on account for rockwork and a further £20 later that year. In 1786 Josiah was paid £25 and in 1787 seven guineas. In 1788 stones and fossils were brought from Bath by Edward Eatwell, a blacksmith, William Mathews and Thomas Angel. On 4 February 1788 Josiah received £18 19s. 9d. and on 22 November the work was completed, Josiah then receiving the sum of £115 17s. 6d., his account having been paid 'in full'. He was asked to come back to Bowood at the end of 1790, perhaps to make a small change, or repairs and was paid a further £1 11s. 6d. This was four years' work for Josiah, but he was well paid, receiving a total over the four years of £190 7s. 3d. plus the £1 11s. 6d.[5]

There are no signs of decorations or fossils on the rockwork of the cascade, but there is considerable additional rockwork adjacent to the path, and perhaps the grottoes at the top and behind the cascade were further decorated, since the Rev. Mr Townsend of Pewsey, a well known mineralogist had apparently formed a collection of 'Cornish Ores and Crystallizations' which were intended to be used for a grotto at Bowood.[6]

Bowood: the cascade and rock work of the grottoes

A description of the cascade survives, written in 1801 by John Britton in his *Beauties of Wiltshire.*

At the bottom of these grounds is a very fine artificial cascade, where the water falls thirty feet perpendicular and presents a scene truly picturesque and grand... Mr Josiah Lane, ... assisted in the formation of this stupendous work; but it was finished under the direction of the present Marquis

This would have been the small boy who fell down it some years before.

Britton goes on to say

Thus completed and daily improving in wildness and picturesque
effect, it stands a flattering monument of the taste and judgement
of all who were concerned in its construction.

The water dashes out of several excavations in the rock; and
the principal sheet, after falling a few yards, dashes against some
projecting masses of stone, and flies off in a cloud of white spray.
The dashing and roar of the waters, the jumbled confusion of the
rocks, the wildness and seclusion of the place, and the various
subterranean passages under the head of the river, conspire to
render it a scene strikingly pleasing to every man of taste; but
more peculiarly so to the painter and admirer of the picturesque;
for here he may indulge himself in the reveries of fancy, and
by a small effort of imagination, may think himself among the
wild waterfalls of North Wales, or the thundering cataracts of
Switzerland.

This cascade is produced by the overflowing water of the
lake; in construction which, the latter was made to expand in its
present consequence. By raising an high embanked head, the
waters have been thrown out of the original channel, and caused
to cover an extent of about thirty acres.

Charles Hamilton had only a few months in which to view and
appreciate Josiah's interpretation of the Tivoli falls at Bowood. He died
in his house in the Royal Crescent on 11 September 1786, having been
in dispute over an additional purchase of land, prompting an unusually
kind comment by the opinionated Horace Walpole in yet another letter
to Lady Ossory on the 28th of September 1786 –

one of my patriarchs of modern gardening has been killed by
Anstey; author of *The Bath Guide*. Mr Hamilton who has built a
house in the Crescent, was also at eighty-three eager in planting a
new garden and wanted some acres, which Anstey, his neighbour,
not so ancient, destined to the same use. Hamilton wrote a warm
letter on their being refused; and Anstey, who does not hate a
squabble in print, as he has more than once shown, discharged
shaft upon shaft against the poor veteran (who) . . ..died of the
volley.[7]

Charles Hamilton had been a huge influence on the careers of Joseph and Josiah Lane. He knew the Beckfords, Henry Hoare and the Lansdownes. Discussion of their work must have taken place amongst these friends and his recommendations seem to have always been followed. Did he also suggest Josiah for the later work at nearby estate of Bowden Park? This is a smaller grotto but attributable to Josiah on grounds of style and its proximity to the work at Bowood.

19

TAKING TEA WITH CHARLES JAMES FOX
AT ST ANN'S HILL

It should certainly not be assumed that Josiah had now turned away from the style of decorative, mystical grottoes he had built with his father. He had simply widened his repertoire. If the client wanted a charming garden building incorporating a grotto with an upstairs tearoom, then Josiah could provide it. And this is precisely what he did at St Ann's Hill, Chertsey in Surrey some time in the 1790s, probably after working at Bowood. Could he, by this time, provide a little sketch of what the building might look like or alternatively, follow a simple drawing provided by the client. Probably both, although no drawing by the Lanes themselves has ever surfaced.

St Ann's Hill, a pretty but quite small Georgian house, with a canopied verandah running along the full width of the house and set in about ninety acres of Surrey pasture and woodland, was the property of Mrs Elizabeth Armistead. She had bought it in 1783 with the help of a mortgage of £2,000 (in fact the full purchase price) loaned to her by the Duke of Marlborough. She had arrived at a situation in life where the Duke of Marlborough would lend her this sort of sum because she had successfully worked her way upwards in society by her charm and beauty, and been much in demand as a *'grande horizontale'* as the French so nicely put it. She started life in July 1750, with the name of Elizabeth Bridget Cane, and her first job was as a model for a London hairdresser. She then worked as a dresser to the actress Mary Robinson at Drury Lane. This exposed her to other possibilities and by the age of 21 she had renamed herself Mrs Elizabeth Armistead and was working as a high-class prostitute, under the protection of the notorious brothel owner Jane Goadsby. This is turn led to a successful career as a courtesan, being kept in turn by Dukes, Earls and Viscounts, and even at one point, the then Prince of Wales, who in 1782 introduced her to the famous Whig politician Charles James Fox.[1] Surprisingly they became platonic friends, eventually lovers and finally in 1795, husband and wife, although the marriage was kept secret for seven years at her request, to protect Fox' political career. Charles James Fox was the son of Henry Fox.

The new Mr and Mrs Fox settled in to St Ann's Hill in 1784 and Fox gradually grew to love the country life, giving up his notorious gambling and womanising for the pleasures of rural existence, reading the newspapers aloud to Mrs Armistead in the mornings, reading the classics, writing, bird watching and gardening. He grew interested in soil structure, in caring for the land and stopped allowing politics to dominate his life.[2] However, he still took part in political debates and it was after making a particularly passionate speech in June 1806 in favour of abolishing the slave trade, that Fox was taken ill. He underwent the horrible technique of 'tapping' when it is said that five gallons of liquid were drained from him 'very fetid and discoloured' together with a mass of blood. This unpleasant procedure was repeated, but sadly for Mrs Armistead, Fox died in the middle of that September.

She went on to live a long life at Chertsey, dying in November 1840 aged over ninety. She left St Ann's Hill and its lovely gardens and land to Fox's great nephews Henry and Charles Fox but it is a measure of her evidently delightful character that she also left legacies to her servants, Martha Tucker, William Yonde, Jane Goome, her cook Sarah Vallen, gardener Scutt and coachman William Woolbridge.[3]

It is good to imagine Fox and Elizabeth companionably taking tea in their pretty little tea house above its shiny grotto. Whilst it no longer really exists, just one wall being left standing, it must have been a particularly charming example of Josiah's work.

Two slender gothick arches on the ground floor provided the entry, with two similar arches on the opposite long wall. The roof of the ground floor displayed yet again the Lane motif of imitation stalactites coated in shiny lapping feldspar and a pattern of black tufa wound its way around and between the stalactites. The walls and supporting pillars were covered in shells and spar and the floor was of geometrically patterned pebbles outlined in brick and white bone. Outside, the building walls and parapet were of flints, and a free standing wooden staircase with a chinoiserie style handrail led to the upstairs room, which, lit by a round-headed casement window, was where Fox and Elizabeth took tea.[4]

Sadly, it was in the 1960s that the teahouse was vandalised, apparently being almost totally destroyed. The simple, elegant Georgian house too has now been demolished and a huge, white modern house replaces it. The site, with its teahouse ruins, is on private land and therefore unavailable to visit.

The date for the little building is not exact – it is referred to as 'the 1790s' and may have been built by Josiah before or after he worked at Ascot Place; it is certainly not too far away. Charles James Fox as a well known politician knew not only many other MPs, but also many members of the aristocracy, so recommendations for Josiah's work were probably easily obtained. In addition, Fox' father Henry Fox was a close friend of Charles Hamilton; they had been at Christ Church College Oxford together and Charles joined Henry on the Grand Tour in 1732.

Charles James was not a handsome man, but apparently a beguiling one, and a splendid orator. He had been something of a dandy, sporting extremely fashionable clothes and leading a very public and dissolute life. As a Whig MP he had supported the idea of the French Revolution, parliamentary reform and independence for America, but he was not always popular, having a reputation for plain speaking and being opposed to an interfering monarchy. How was he viewed by the quiet, hard-working Josiah? Could it be that Fox was liberal minded enough to talk to workmen, or did his liberality only extend to *his* peers or other similar intellectuals? Even Horace Walpole seems to have nothing to say on this subject. Did Josiah return to Wiltshire with his head full of new ideas? He had certainly had the opportunity of working for and meeting one of the country's great political men, and his even more fascinating wife. This must surely have affected Josiah's thoughts and views. Keeping one's ears, eyes and mind open could provide a wide education.

20

STANDING STONES, TOWERS AND
UMBRAGEOUS GROTS

For hundreds of years the Arundell family had owned a large swathe of the Wiltshire countryside, including the villages of Ansty, Semley, Fovant, Donhead St Mary, Donhead St Andrew, Wardour and most of Tisbury, including the magnificent medieval Place Farm with its huge barn and Court House. These lands had been granted to the family by Henry VIII following the Dissolution of the Monasteries, which ended the ownership by the Abbess of the great Benedictine Abbey of Shaftesbury. This grant was surprising, since the Arundell family held fast to their Catholic faith, and intended that the nuns of Shaftesbury Abbey remain. However, Sir Thomas Arundell was married to Margaret, sister of Henry's fourth wife Catherine Howard, so he had some influence at Court. The family's fortunes subsequently waxed and waned, but in spite of the confiscation of Wardour by the Crown and its subsequent return to the family by Lord Pembroke in exchange for the village of Fovant, the family retained possession of their great estate until the twentieth century, and part of it today. It was asserted in the later, Victorian period that 80% of all the Catholics in Wiltshire at the time lived on the estate of the Arundells. A powerful family indeed.

By the late 1700s the 8th Earl of Arundell had built a magnificent new mansion, designed by James Paine, on a high area of Wardour overlooking the ruins of the family's old Wardour Castle. This old castle, which had suffered a siege and subsequent retrieval from the Parliamentarians during the Civil War, was now a romantic ruin, sitting in the remains of its formal gardens. Catholic priests, who had lived hidden in the surrounding woodlands were now able to emerge and Mass could be held in the new chapel at the mansion, a place of great beauty, the interior being designed by Sir John Soane. From the new enormous Georgian mansion (the largest Georgian house in Wiltshire), built between 1771 and 1776, the view towards the ruin provided the picturesque landscape so sought after by the fortunate landowners of the period. The Earl decided, having sought the advice of Capability Brown and Richard Woods on the landscaping, that all it lacked was a grotto to enhance the view back to the house from the ruin, where the good fortune of his great family could be contemplated in tranquillity.

Luckily for the Earl, he not only had access to Josiah Lane, now at home in Tisbury, he also had his eye on some splendid stones, standing in one of his own fields close to Place Farm barn. It is said that the stones were in Lost Stone Field, but that name is a corruption of an earlier one, Low Stone Field. The precise site of the small henge is not properly identified, but the instructions to Josiah and his team were to

Wardour Castle: the main grotto

The Standing Stones and alcoves at Wardour Castle

lift these stones and take them over to old Wardour Castle to form part of a grotto.

This was an Herculean task. The stones, set in a small vallum, a banked circle, were said to be twenty feet in height but this dimension may refer to their total height including the part which had been buried The three standing stones were, according to Colt Hoare, at the centre of the vallum, which was also set round with stones.[1] The three central stones were placed to form three sides of a square. In the centre of the square, during the excavation of the stones, Josiah's team found a skeleton, which was carefully lifted and apparently reburied at Wardour.

Tastes in gardening had changed and the Earl wanted to be up to date, so he requested a natural looking grotto, no decorations of shells or corals, no feldspar, no glitter. Josiah set to work to establish the main grotto on a raised terrace, to be reached by a flight of wide, shallow stone steps set round with gloomy yews. This was opposite the main entrance to the castle ruin, above what had been the bowling green. This site enabled him to build what looks like a rough, natural group of rocks of honey-combed limestone, with a number of entrances, some hidden, leading to dark tunnels. The grotto was built on a structure of bricks, covered in the tufa like limestone rocks, and although Josiah used a few ammonites, since they are locally very available, the rest of the grotto is undecorated. The tunnels allow for sudden glimpses out through rough apertures, and the different levels gradually lead the visitor to a flat area on the top of the grotto, which at that time would have enabled the visitor to view the lake below the castle, the linked ponds along the valley, and to look across parkland to the main, new mansion.

To the left of the main grotto, a short walk along the terrace brings the visitor to a further group of stones, a 'rock shelter' of semi-circular shape, with a central Gothic arch providing a covered seat. At least two of the large standing stones to the right of the arch may well be the ones from Place Farm and this seems to be a suitable spot for the reburial of the Neolithic skeleton.

The whole area, castle ruin, the lawns, yews, grottoes, terraces, lakes, ponds and the frisson of the buried skeleton, provide a wonderfully romantic ensemble, further enhanced by the gothick banqueting house within the castle bailey, above the lower edge of its substantial walls. The design of this is attributed to Mr Lancelot Brown.

By the time Josiah had finished work at Wardour, he had settled back into village life, getting to know his old friends again, most of whom must by now have been married with children. He may already have known Rebekah Mould from an earlier time, but she was nine years younger than him, so maybe he had not noticed her before. Rebekah, who was not very well educated (she could not sign her name), came from a very large family, with branches all over the local villages. Her parents were Joseph and Mary Mould who lived in Fonthill Gifford, where Rebekah was born in 1762.[2]

In early 1794 Rebekah found she was pregnant (the Lanes seem to have had a habit of getting the girlfriend pregnant first and then marrying) and she and Josiah married on 28 April in Tisbury, a couple of months before baby Tabatha was born, the baby being baptised in Tisbury on the 10th June.[3] Since the Burton family was probably already in residence in the cottage in Hindon Lane which Josiah had inherited (they were certainly there by 1798 according to the Land Tax Redemption records) perhaps he and Rebekah rented nearby, unless they moved in with his sister Rebeckah at Jerrards in Fonthill Gifford.

This was convenient, because Josiah went back to working at Fonthill for young William Beckford, who had once again returned to Fonthill from abroad, this time from Paris, for a short stay at home. Beckford was off to the continent again quite quickly, to Lisbon, where he occupied his time with designing a Portugese Gothic style house. Presumably during that short period at Fonthill, he asked Josiah to continue work at Fonthill, on the grottoes on the eastern side of the lake again, where the trees had grown to maturity. Beckford, with advice from his old tutor John Lettice, arranged for border planting along the lakeside walks, allowing the rocks, mosses and ferns to anchor the effects. This was Beckford's 'Alpine Garden'. The grotto was planted with violets, ivy, periwinkles and wallflowers. The bathhouse was encrusted with shells and coral, and in summer the planted semi-wild flowers gave way to sunken pots of lilies, jasmine, tuberoses and orange trees, so the area was always perfumed and flowery.

All this was to enhance the magical mystical experience for the visitor, but little luxuries were not forgotten, when Henry Meister, a French visitor to Fonthill in 1793 arrived, his group of friends were treated to 'a table covered with pineapples, grapes and other refreshments in gold and china vases'.

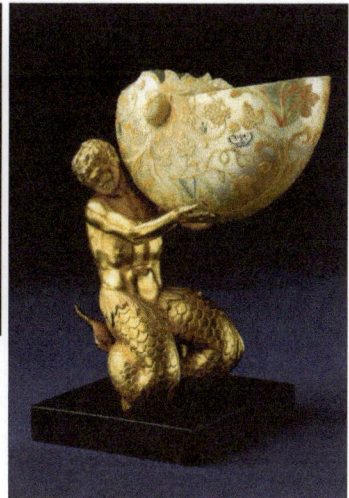

From the William Beckford Collection, cups and saucers by Dihl &Guerhard factory, and Nautilus shell in ivory, silver gilt and marble, engraved by Cornelius Van Belleken

Meister also mentions that during his walk along the banks of the lake, he visited 'a temple dedicated to Hercules, built on a small eminence'. This would seem to refer to the caverns high above the lakeside, in the Alpine Garden, where Josiah had his workshop. Hercules probably refers to the broken statue that lay in one of the caves, and is one of the odd pieces of statuary that may simply have been dumped there by Beckford after his father's death, when the style of the gardens was being altered. The caves are connected by a passage running along

the back, and Josiah would clearly have needed a sheltered place to work
the stones he cut from the nearby quarry, and to keep any larger bits of
his quarrying tools.

The Fonthill landscape had long been thought to be a magical,
even spiritual place. It has been suggested that Milton's landscape in
Book IV of Paradis Lost was based upon Fonthill:

> Betwixt them lawns, or level downs, and flocks
> Grazing the tender herb, were interpos'd,
> Or palmy hillock; or the flow'ry lap
> Of some irriguous valley spread her store,
> Flow'rs of all hue and without thorn the rose;
> Another side, umbrageous grots and caves
> Of cool recess, o'er which the mantling vine
> Lays forth her purple grape and gently creeps
> Luxuriant. Meanwhile murmuring waters fall
> Down the slope hills, dispers'd, or in a lake,
> That to the fringed bank with myrtle crown'd
> Her crystal mirror holds, unite their streams

This seems to anticipate a future Fonthill since Milton was writing
in the 1660s. Young William however would no doubt have been made
familiar with Paradise Lost and its subsequent classical imagery of
Pan dancing with the Graces and the Hours among the flowers could
well have been part of the inspirations for his improvements to the old
Fonthill landscape.

Working in that quiet place, did Joseph or Josiah experience the
presence of the gods? They had no classical education but overhearing
conversations, imagining the dancing nymphs, hearing the pipes of Pan
in the sounds of trickling water, or sheep bells – perhaps Josiah dreamt
of a goddess frolicking in his spring fed bathing pool. This place was as
much his and his father's landscape as it was the Beckfords'. He leaves
his initials in one of the caverns in the Alpine Garden, carving into a
roundel:

J. L. 1794

When Fonthill is sold, and Mr Mortimer's nephew builds his
woollen mill below the lake, with its surrounding cottages, the valley
becomes a small industrial site. The sound of sheep bells is drowned by

the clangour of the machinery and the loud sounds of men and women working, shouting above the manufacturing din. It takes time for the valley to heal after the mill declines and falls, and for Pan to return, to be seen peeping through the trees, his music drifting across the glittering green water of the lake.

There is one final part of the Lanes' work at Fonthill - the 'viewing tower ' on the western side of the lake above the old boat house, looking out across the lake towards the new landing stage, the lakeside walks and the grottoes. This tower, sometimes referred to as a cromlech, is built in Josiah's best naturalistic style and may have been built to replace his father's 'Umbrella' seat. There is a small, low, rough interior ground floor room, undecorated, which may have been designed as a special

Fonthill Estate: the viewing tower overlooking the lake

retreat for Beckford's dwarf, and steps outside lead up to a viewing platform, now infested with tree growths. Josiah had just finished the flat viewing area at the top of the Wardour grotto, so perhaps the tower was built at his suggestion. The tower, sadly, was already damaged by 1823 when Rutter and Britton were writing about Fonthill, but it remains today, a sturdy ruin, defiantly surviving with its wild hairstyle of bare branches in winter and a crown of green leaves in summer.

In 1796 Beckford returned from Portugal, with his head full of ideas for a monumental Gothic Abbey on the highest point of his estate, to be greeted on his return by the brass band of the Fonthill Volunteers, who played for him, marching up and down on his lawn at Fonthill Splendens.[4] Although he was now largely forgiven for his pecadilloes, not all his neighbours felt the same, and he was cold shouldered by Lord Radnor at a dinner in Salisbury that year. Beckford however, managed to seem oblivious to any disapproval, and carried on with the plans for the Abbey, all thoughts of grottoes now jettisoned. To the very great pleasure of the stonemasons, carpenters, plumbers, glaziers and labourers of Tisbury, Fonthill and the surrounding villages, William Beckford commissioned work to start on the building of his greatest achievement, Fonthill Abbey, with its massively tall spire. The foundations, if in fact there were any, were to be laid in the winter of 1796. The monastic style Gothic building would, Beckford hoped, restore him to his rightful position as a respectable, successful and recognised member of society, thereby gaining him the peerage he felt had been denied him (or which he had himself squandered, depending upon your point of view) in 1784. James Wyatt was to be his architect. Wyatt had recently been appointed Surveyor-General and Comptroller of the Office of Works, and was asked to design a most magnificent Gothic style abbey/palace for Beckford, who could then fill it with works of art, ceramics, silver and gold chalices, objets d'art and suitably extravagant furniture.

Beckford could hardly wait for it all to be finished, and as he was still the richest man in England, why should he have to wait? Work went ahead at full speed, and Wyatt had to encourage the workers to move fast in order to satisfy his client. There is no specific record of the views of the local masons and bricklayers at this stage, and no doubt they were all delighted to have the work, failing to express their doubts as to the building's ultimate safety. Indeed, would anyone have believed them?

On 6 January 1797 Beckford celebrated the progress of the work with a Twelfth Night Festival for the local gentry and, it is said, eleven thousand local peasantry, who all attended at Fonthill Splendens, where two huge bonfires burned on the lawns, a Turkish tent was provided for the gentry and a marquee erected for the peasantry, with seven long tables inside, each seating one hundred people.[5] A special place for the children was arranged. Oxen and sheep were barbecued, bread and strong beer provided and after lunch there were wrestling matches, races and single stick contests. A football match followed, in which, it was reported, many of the crowd took as much part as the two teams who were supposed to be in the match.

In an excess of enthusiasm and largesse towards the locals, Beckford distributed two hundred warm blankets and a load of fuel to each poor family in the two Fonthill villages, besides a sum of money to 'the indigent'. No doubt all this bounty was really welcomed, particularly since this was the year in which rioting occurred in other parts of the county due to weavers' incomes being reduced as a result of the introduction of labour saving machinery. A wonderful day was enjoyed by all, and the workers could rejoice with the thought that for the new few years at least there would be food on the table for their families.

No doubt Josiah too had a great day with all his family, but he would not be working at the new Abbey, or on the Fonthill landscape as he had received news that he was wanted near London again, at Ascot Place, where the owner had decided, having seen the Lane's work at Oatlands and Painshill, that he too needed a splendid grotto in his newly acquired property. Josiah saddled up his horse, and bagged up his tools. Leaving Rebekah and baby Tabatha, he rode off towards London once more.

21

ICICLES AT ASCOT

Ascot Place has had a variety of owners since the house was built in the early 18th century. These have included the baked beans tycoon 'Jack' Heinz II, the Mercedes Benz heir Mick Flick, and William Lidderdale a governor of the Bank of England. It is currently in the ownership of the royal family of a Middle Eastern country. Its proximity to London and easy access from London's main air terminal, closeness to the Royal racecourse, the 400 acres of Berkshire countryside and wonderful landscaped garden make it a desirable retreat for the very rich. As a private property, and with the estate surrounded by a 6'6"wall, it is now impossible to access the grotto unless an invitation is issued.

Daniel Agace, the son or grandson of Zachary Agace a successful Huguenot master weaver, obtained Ascot Place in 1787, which he bought by a decree in Chancery because of the bankruptcy and death of its previous owner Andrew Lindegren, for whom the house itself had been built. Mr Agace concentrated on the grounds, building a circular Corinthian Temple and, at one end of a canal, the grotto and cascade, the former in much the same style as those at Painshill and Oatlands Park. There have been suggestions that the design was by Mr Agace himself and the construction by 'Turnbull, a Scotch mason'. Other sources have suggested it is by Thomas Sandby. However, the interior of the grotto is apparently so similar to those at Painshill and Oatlands that it is logical to assume that Ascot Place, too, is the work of the Lane family, although now it is Josiah on his own who is responsible. Mike Cousins puts Ascot Place grotto as either being built during 1789-91 or possibly started later, in 1795[1]

From the house, the grotto can be seen across the lake, as a large pile of rocks with a cave opening. It is approached by a small humped back bridge, where the rocks from which it is built can be seen beside the cascade. At the top of the artificial mound there is a crown of rock concealing the octagon window which lights the interior of the grotto. Descending to lake level, the visitor reaches the entrance of sarsen stones, presumably brought from the Berkshire Downs. From a drawing of the exterior in 1813, it can be deduced that the style has become a little more rustic and heavy, with the solidity of the sarsen stones marking the entrance. The structure is of bricks and mortar, with the inner walls lime rendered and decorated with slag, flint, tufa and clinker, all coated with a lime wash. A slag lined passage leads to the domed central quatrefoil chamber, lit by a glazed octagonal lantern window in the roof. The main chamber is 35' long, with narrow tunnels leading from this to other smaller chambers. Wooden benches are set

Ascot Place, Berkshire: the central room of the grotto (left), and ceiling details (right), both photographed by Barbara Jones, c. 1953

into the stone walls. Carefully designed pebble floors have inset pools, one under a magnificent rocky arch which has a ten foot span. Two of the pools have pedestals, which may have been small fountains, or were designed to hold sculptures. Each room is of an irregular shape, but the asymmetry is contrived to appear natural and unplanned. The interior is much as Oatlands is described, but its pendant ceiling icicles of uneven lengths are even more sharply defined. Flint decorates the lower parts of the walls to dado rail height and cut oblongs of mica and glittering white quartz crystals soar upwards to the ceiling, where the now familiar zig-zag star pattern, this time executed in red quartz, surrounds the sharp stalactites of crystal covered cones. The ceiling and those of the smaller rooms are intended to be illuminated by candles set in niches, by the light coming in through the high lantern windows and by tiny skylights.

All the above information is taken from a report by a member of the conservation team which restored the grotto in 2011 and from Barbara Jones' description in *Grottoes and Follies* first published in 1953.[2] She was lucky enough to have visited Ascot Place, probably in the 1940s, taking photographs and drawing the interior. She comments that the grotto was lit by white and red electric light bulbs, 'an effect' she comments, 'which the 18th century would have loved'.[3]

This grotto, a return to the style of work that Josiah learned from his father, is one of the last of the great decorative, rococo flourishes of the picturesque garden. After this, with the exception of the lost grotto at Norbiton, grottoes reflected the changing ideas of the later part of the century, the desire for a more natural, wilder and more craggy landscape, less decoration in the grottoes, a much more savage, monumental, Neolithic-style approach, to which Josiah was well able to respond.

Ascot Place grotto is listed as a Grade I building under the Planning (Listed Buildings and Conservation Areas) Act 1990, so although it is not possible for ordinary members of the public to see it, at least the grotto is being cared for. Garden historians Headley and Meulenkamp have commented that 'it is hard to think of a finer grotto in Britain' and it is an outstanding example of a Rococo garden structure related to an important landscape. It is acknowledged to be a superb example of Lane workmanship.

22

MR TURNER, BOWDEN PARK
AND BELCOMBE COURT

The end of the 18th century was approaching, the French had revolted and were at war with England. Inflation hit the country and families were not only expected to manage on reduced wages, but very often their sons were press-ganged into the Army or the Navy, depriving families of working age young men. House rentals rose again and there were food shortages. Landowners were better off, with Enclosures Acts being drawn up and becoming effective, so some people were flourishing.

The health of the population did not improve however, and in June 1797 little Tabatha died, aged just three.[1] Of course it is impossible to know the cause of her death and although the deaths of young children were still common, it did not make acceptance any easier, particularly for Josiah and Rebekah, who were older parents, Josiah now 44 and Rebekah 35 and who perhaps had hoped but not expected to have children. It was therefore doubly hard for them.

In Wylye, which is not far away from Tisbury, Josiah's sister Deborah, who had married Stephen Titt in 1775, lived in a comfortable property owned by Josiah, which was valued for Land Tax Redemption Act purposes at £2 12s. 11d. p.a., rather more than his Tisbury cottage, but there may have been more land attached to the Wylye house.[2]

Deborah and Stephen by now have had three children, another Stephen, John and the youngest, little Deborah, born in 1796. Josiah's sister and her husband, according to one of the Titt family tombstones in the churchyard of St Mary the Virgin at Wylye, also lost a little girl named Tabitha, and an earlier Deborah, in 1777. Deborah's surviving children and grandchildren went on to a prosperous future, one branch moving to Tisbury in the mid 19th century, her grandson eventually becoming the proprietor of the Beckford Arms, farming a few acres and having a number of children, quite a few servants and a number of labourers. Her middle child, John, produced three children and some grandchildren and remained in the house in Wylye. There are at least six Titt family tombstones in the churchyard there, all the tombstones being grouped together in a prominent position. The Titt family clearly became of some importance in the village.

Deborah's youngest child, little Deborah, moved to Tisbury to marry John Burton in 1815, and to live in Josiah's second property, where she remained until her death in 1860.[3]

Josiah's sister Rebeckah Lane, who married Stephen Spencer on 29 November 1786, now had two sons, Josiah Spencer born 9 May 1787 and Isace Spencer, born 10 June 1794.[4] (Isace is the way his name is spelt on the Parish Register). They were still living in Jerrards, at Fonthill Gifford, at the end of the century, although for the purposes of the Land Tax Redemption Act 1798, Stephen Spencer is listed as both owner and occupier, presumably because upon marrying, Rebeckah's inheritance of Jerrards and her £100 had become the property of her husband.[5]

So there were at least five little Lane descendants, and in Spring 1799 Josiah and Rebekah have another little daughter. However, sadly this little Tabitha dies almost immediately and it is another two years before they have any more children. In May 1801 Rebekah is delivered of twins, Joseph Hambleton Lane and yet another Tabitha, both baptised in Tisbury on the 26th May 1801.[6]

There is a last glimpse of Josiah working at Fonthill and it is the only picture that just might be of him. In 1799 the artist JMW Turner returned to Fonthill to paint the Abbey. He had already visited briefly earlier, producing a watercolour of the intermediate design of the Abbey by James Wyatt and now on his later visit he was accompanied by Wyatt and a group of other artists, Henry Tresham, William Hamilton and Benjamin West, and they stayed for three weeks. During this time Turner painted a number of large watercolours including 'View of Fonthill

JMW Turner 1799/80 East View of Fonthill Abbey from the Quarry,
National Gallery

from a stone quarry'. In this painting the Abbey looms impressively over the Wiltshire landscape, its ultimate height on the horizon surely exaggerated. In the foreground the quarry on the eastern side of the lake shows stonemasons and a thatched shelter amongst the rocks. To the left and right are groups of the trees planted earlier by the Alderman and below, what appears to be a winding path leading down to a misty lake. The sky is a golden and pink wash, so we can imagine Turner sitting at the top of the quarry all afternoon, waiting to catch the western evening light on the stones and the trees, and for it to cast heavy shadows on the foreground rocks before him. It is to be hoped that Josiah is one of the stonemasons in the middle distance left, working in the evening sunshine in the environment he made his own.

Now Josiah was offered work in the north of the County again, probably through the Fonthill connection, since it was to work for a successful Jamaican plantation and slave owner, Barnard Dickenson.

Close to Lacock Abbey and convenient for the London to Bath road is the very pretty estate of Bowden Park, which sits elegantly on top of a steep hill, surrounded by lawns, woodland and Bowden Common. Before the mid 1700s the land was owned by the Fane family, then George Johnson MP for Devizes. It was bought in 1751 by Mr Ezekiel Dickenson of Monks House, Corsham, for his son Barnard Dickenson

Bowden Park Wiltshire: exterior of grotto with Gothic window

Bowden Park: grotto ceiling details

who was only six years old at the time. In 1796, Barnard, now a rich 50 year old, employed James Wyatt to design and build for him an elegant classical mansion. The grounds were to be landscaped in the current style and Barnard decided he had to have a grotto, which should look down across the sweeping lawns to the valley below. Josiah, being well known to Barnard's near neighbour at Bowood, was the fashionable person's grotto builder, so sometime around the turn of the century Josiah gets on his horse again and leaves Rebekah with the new babies to go to work at Bowden. There were plenty of estate cottages, so no doubt he was able to acquire somewhere to rent or board quite easily.

This grotto combines the delicacy of the Lanes' earlier work with Josiah's later monumental style. Pretty Gothic double doors open into a large central space, the uneven, domed ceiling decorated once again with fine, and this time, very thin stalactites, with a looping pattern of black stones wandering in and out of the needle-like stalactites. The walls are intricately covered with shells and corals. Some of the shells are English razors and cockles. Huge corals and pink conches add to the frivolity and a band of ammonites defines or nearly defines the base of the walls where they meet the floor.[7] The purple, green and gold glass in the gothic arches of the windows creates a depth of watery light and shadow. As the grotto is sited to catch the western setting sun, it lights up in the evenings, intensifying the effect of the golden, glittering glass and the crystals. Josiah could still create the interior magic he learned with his father at Painshill. Side wings built from Cyclopean slabs of greeny- pink sandstone contain smaller grotto spaces and the tunnel to the right winds narrowly away to exit at the rear of the building, which is free standing.

Barnard Dickenson had continued to add to his fortunes, by now being the joint owner of seven sugar plantations in Jamaica, all staffed by his slaves. In 1814 he died, leaving a huge fortune; his wife's marriage settlement share reverted to her (£13,000 approximately) plus she was to have the interest on further £12,000 and the right to live at Bowden Park for her lifetime. His nephews Ezekiel and Jeremiah received half each of his 'Jamaican lands and enslaved people' and his property in Fenchurch Street.[8] A further large sum was provided for his niece Elizabeth and he left legacies for his staff in England, and to Bath Hospital and Salisbury Infirmary. It is interesting that on one hand he could leave money for hospitals in England, quite a charitable thing to do, but that he could also pass on the ownership of people, i.e. slaves, as property. With the abolition of slavery looming, now doubt the nephews were glad to have the Fenchurch Street property. It is not known how much Josiah earned from building the Bowden Park grotto. Bowden Park opens its gardens to the public under the National Gardens Scheme once a year, usually in May.

The last two grottoes associated with the Lanes are Belcombe Court in Bradford on Avon, again in Wiltshire, which still exists, very well cared for in its elegant 18th century garden setting, but for which there is no definite attribution to Josiah, and Norbiton House, which no longer exists, but which is definitely attributed to him.

Belcombe Court was the home and, to some extent, the workplace of Francis Yerbury a Bradford on Avon clothier, who employed weavers in both Trowbridge and Bradford on Avon. He had trained as a barrister, but whilst undergoing training in London during the early part of the century he became fascinated by the weaving techniques used by the Huguenot silk weavers of Spitalfields. He quickly realised that the coarse woven cloths of the West Country could be improved by these different techniques and so successfully introduced a lightweight, superfine woven twill with a silky soft feel, to be known as a 'cassimere'. The original cashmere had been expensive to produce as it was woven from the wonderfully soft hair of Kashmiri goats. Yerbury experimented and found he could produce a soft summerweight twill, weighing only 7oz. for a yard of standard width of fabric, by his revised technique and his company began producing this in 1769. He soon became a very rich man, enabling him to improve the house and park his father John had bought on the north bank of the river, above Bradford on Avon. Francis, who had owned this property since his father's death in 1728, commissioned John Wood the Elder, the architect of Bath, to enlarge the old house and its outbuildings, which were to be used as offices and workspaces for the business according to the architect himself.

In 1778 John William Yerbury inherited the cloth making business and the estate. Spinning, fulling, weaving and dyeing had traditionally provided a secondary, home based employment for the small farmers and labourers of the clayland areas of North and West Wiltshire, and this was an important source of additional income from what was handcrafted work which could be done at home, when as labourers they were not needed on the land, and therefore not earning. Bradford on Avon and Trowbridge were two of the small towns which thrived and became prosperous through cloth making. However, the introduction of the spinning jenny and of carding machines caused problems for workers, reducing the number of people required to make the cloth, and reducing incomes. Rioting occurred in both Trowbridge and Bradford when machines were burned and the mobs had to be dispersed by the militia.

In 1787 about fifteen hundred weavers from the Trowbridge and Bradford on Avon area, having had some success in persuading some employers not to implement new regulations, tried to force their way into Bradford. At Belcombe Court they were stopped in their tracks by Mr Yerbury, who showed them, from the windows of his house, two small patereroes (small cannon on swivel action mounts) with which he could aim at any position across his extensive lawns. Supported by many armed friends, and his useful small cannons, he addressed the rioters and persuaded them to disperse. By the time the militia arrived the following day, the rioters had, unsurprisingly, all gone quietly home. Also unsurprisingly, given the force of his personality, Mr Yerbury's fortunes continued to flourish and he indulged himself with improvements to his delightful garden and parkland, including the building of the compulsory, still fashionable grotto. There is no direct archival evidence that Josiah was responsible for this one, but in style it is convincingly a Lane creation, and in particular a later Josiah one.[9]

Belcombe Court, Bradford upon Avon, grotto exterior

Belcombe Court grotto, looking out towards the pavilion

Free standing, it is a picturesque pile of rocks, seemingly a natural heap of holey limestone, beside a formal, but slightly curving pond. The entrance, to the right, is a serpentine, creepy, very dark passage leading to an oval room, with a jagged, open arch looking out over the pond to a classical rotunda of ashlar limestone standing on a raised grassy mound. This rotunda, built by a local stonemason much earlier in the 18th century, was much despised by John Wood the Elder when he was building the house.[10] Looking through the grotto arch, the view is partially obscured by a stone monolith, which appears to be just about holding up the roof by the point of its apex. Inside the grotto is a curved stone bench, but the walls are not decorated, nor is the ceiling, although this is of spars of rock, some small and some of a reasonable depth, pointing downwards. The only real decoration lies on the floor, in the form of inset broken ammonite whirls. The floor is green and damp, with trickling water from the pond, an ideal place for frogs to nestle amongst the ammonites. Perhaps Dr Johnson was right when asked whether he thought a grotto was an admirable place, he replied that indeed it was, 'for toads'. Again, the ammonites may well have come from the Tisbury area, but John William Yerbury himself was a great fossil collector, leaving 'all monies and goods, including a fossil

collection' to his sons on his death in 1824.[11] There is no secondary exit
to this grotto and the visitor must retrace his careful steps back through
the excessively narrow passage, avoiding banging his head on the low
roof. Above the lower chamber is a small open balcony edged with
rough stones, known as the Banqueting Room, although any banquet
held there would have had to be a small and rather intimate experience.

The grotto is now sheltered by mature shrubbery and clipped
trees, and softened by tiny ferns and little plants. The whole ensemble is

Belcombe Court, the grotto floor encrusted with ammonites

reflected in the still water of the pond,
with its water lilies and huge carp,
creating a formal but particularly pretty
setting for such a Neolithic looking
building. It is similar in exterior and
interior style to Wardour, and in its
setting to Bowden Park - a folly to
enhance this delightful intimate,
stage-set of a garden. It would be
unreasonable to suggest that it is not

*Ammonite subdichotomacerus, from
the Etches collection*

the work of Josiah and if so, may well date from around 1810. There is further rockwork in the northern part of the park, carved into the cliff face and having stone seats in two caves and a further larger circular cave, but there is no evidence that this is the work of Josiah, or when this work was done. More research might reveal further information but Belcombe Court is a private house, and the garden is only open very occasionally.

23

'FRITTERED AWAY ITS BEAUTY BY
GROTTOES, HERMITAGES . . .'

In 1804 a 43 year old clergyman-poet was granted the living of Bremhill, a small northern Wiltshire village. The same year saw him appointed as a prebendary of Salisbury Cathedral. William Lisle Bowles had been writing poetry since his student days at Trinity College, Oxford where he won the Chancellor's Prize for Latin Verse. After graduation in 1786, he hoped to obtain a fellowship, but this failed to happen and, like many members of his distinguished Wiltshire family, he took Holy Orders and became Curate at Donhead St Andrew, (a village close to Tisbury), where both his grandfather and his uncle had held the living. At the time of William's appointment, the Rev. John Benett, the brother of Mr Benett of Pyt House Tisbury, was the Rector. William Lisle Bowles' parents, the Rev. William Thomas Bowles MA and his wife Bridget, both lived and died in Shaftesbury and William's brother Charles Bowles became Recorder of Shaftesbury and worked with Sir Richard Colt Hoare on the History of Modern Wiltshire.

The Bowles family name was extensive in the north Dorset, southern Wiltshire area and even Joseph and Josiah had a Bowles relative – Joseph's mother Sarah was the daughter of Mary and Henry Bowles of Shaftesbury, and she was born in that town. The Bowles worked in a number of professions, the clergy, one was a surgeon, another an innkeeper, another a glover, and there were two prominent Freemasons in the town of Shaftesbury by the name of Bowles. Amongst the parcels of land owned by the extended Lane family was Bowles Close in Hindon Lane Tisbury. So, local connections for the Rev. William Lisle Bowles, but of a different social class to that of the Lanes, and there appears to be no direct relationship.

William Bowles was known as a mild mannered, eccentric gentleman, absent minded, very musical with antiquarian interests. His poetry, while not considered to be of the first rank, brought him some acclaim. His early sonnets, being inspired by his love of nature, had been much appreciated by the young Samuel Taylor Coleridge, and by Charles Lamb and William Wordsworth. His later, epic ballads did not find favour with the established critics and are now hardly known at all. He had become too wordy, losing the focus and gentle beauty of his earlier work. However, although a kindly man, he thought highly of his own abilities and after editing a ten volume edition of the work of Alexander Pope, in 1806, he became embroiled in a bitter dispute with Lord Byron over his literary criticism which Byron saw as the devaluation of Pope's work. The tenacious Rev. Bowles did not change his opinions and a long and unhappy series of pamphlets and letters were published by both parties.

This confidence in his own abilities is reflected in the alterations Bowles made to the parsonage at Bremhill, where his initials appear in various prominent positions on the stonework of the house and on one of his sculptural additions to the renovated garden. As an antiquarian he had no qualms about removing interesting pieces of Gothic style stonework from the nearby ruins of Stanley Abbey, a Cistercian monastery founded in 1154, and inserting them into the renovations. The parsonage (now known as Bremhill Court) is of 15th century origin, extended in the 17th century and considerably 'improved' by William Bowles with Gothic style additions, turrets, pinnacles and parapet. He had the gardens redesigned in the by then rather old fashioned style of Mr William Shenstone at Leasowes in Shropshire, but according to Bowles' close friend the Irish poet Thomas Moore, he 'frittered away its beauty by grottoes, hermitages and Shenstonian inscriptions'. So, with Bowles' connections and Bremhill's close proximity to Bowood Park, could his grottoes be designed or built by Josiah Lane?

Bremhill is situated close to Bowood House and William soon became a welcome member of the social life surrounding the Marquess of Lansdowne, invited to parties and meeting the writers, scientists and intellectuals who formed the circle of the Lansdowne's friends and acquaintances. It is reported that on one occasion William fell and broke his arm when rushing to make the acquaintance of Madame de Stael. He apparently picked himself up and professed that he would be happy to suffer even more pain in order to have the pleasure of meeting her. He probably met Lancelot Brown there and would certainly have viewed Josiah's work on the cascade, grottoes and hermitage in the park.

William had been disappointed in love as a young man, the parents of the young lady he fell in love with feeling he was an unsuitable match for their daughter. William went travelling after this unfortunate event, to the wilds of northern England and Scotland then to the Rhine. The poet Thomas Gray had recommended regular travel to the Highlands for poets, painters, gardeners and clergymen (in that order) for if they did not 'their imagination can be made up of nothing but bowling greens, flowering shrubs, horse ponds, fleet ditches, shell grottoes and Chinee rails'. Bowles would certainly have recognised himself in three of Thomas Gray's categories, and perhaps his imagination was inspired by his travels, for on his return he wrote his first, successful, volume of sonnets.

In 1797 he found some happiness in his marriage to Magdalen Wake, but they had no children. Mrs Bowles enjoyed teaching the poor children of Bremhill parish and on each Sunday they would be instructed by her, in summer on the lawn of the parsonage. Perhaps lemonade and buns were provided as a suitable incentive to attendance. They learnt William's specially written little poems in *The Little Villager's Verse Book*. It must have been delightful place to be, with the sheep grazing in the field below the garden ha- ha, their bells tuned, apparently, to fourths and fifths to please the musical William. His reputation as a local Rector was good and he composed suitably poetic epitaphs for the tombstones of members of his congregation. This comfortable rural existence was exchanged each year for the excitements of the City of Salisbury where, first as prebendary and then as Canon, William was required to stay for three months of each year. He particularly enjoyed the musical life of the cathedral.

Nevertheless he found plenty of time to indulge his gardening pleasures at Bremhill. To one side of the house there is a 100 yard

Standing stones at Bremhill Court, Wiltshire

archery allee, which is a pleasant green walk, and must surely date to a much earlier period, below which the ground slopes down quite sharply to a small tree- shaded lake. William arranged for the water from springs above the parsonage to collect in level stone rills, enabling the water to flow down over a small cascade into the lake. The cascade is not large, or high, and is now smooth, unlike Josiah's rocky creations, but beside the cascade can be seen the remains of a rocky wall, perhaps a retaining or back wall for something larger. It is of a tufa like stone, but now totally overgrown. Around this area, which is very slightly flattened, are a number of standing stones, seemingly placed at random and although the site is absolutely ideal for a grotto with a trickling water feature, it is now difficult to imagine how the existing placing of the stones would have worked as part of a grotto. William, as an antiquarian, might simply have wanted standing stones, but these are sited in a wooded dell just a few feet above water level, whereas a standing stone circle or henge would have been better seen from the terrace, in an open field position. William would certainly have known and probably visited the great Avebury stone circle, the Avenue and the long barrow at Kennet. Sarsen stones were still laying like sleeping sheep on the downs around nearby Marlborough. The nearby newly built canal may well have been utilised to bring a few of these close to his Bremhill property.

Two semi-circular tufa like stone seats adorned the garden – these may have been the 'hermitages' referred to by Bowles' Irish friend Thomas Moore, who was also a member of the Bowood social circle, a poet himself, and who lived at nearby Devizes. The rougher stones from these seats have been reused in walls at Bremhill, and are visible as different textured stone from the more formal cut stone of the rest of the buildings and may have been brought to the property, again possibly via the canal but perhaps from the opposite direction, i.e. the quarries at Bath.

From the garden at Bremhill an impressive obelisk on the Bowood skyline can be seen and William paid his respects to this by erecting a stone obelisk in his own garden, in line with the Bowood obelisk. William's obelisk commemorates the peace of March 1814 after Napoleon's banishment to Elba. Of course, William adds his own initials to the base of his obelisk.

This cultured cleric, living as he and his wife did, among the illustrious upper social circles of Wiltshire, and having such an interest in nature, music and antiquarian pursuits, would seem to be the ideal patron for Josiah. The fact that it is recorded that there were 'grottoes and hermitages' in his garden make it seem possible that Josiah might have had a hand in beautifying the Reverend's surroundings. Alas, the remains, while suggestive of grotto-like stonework, seem far more likely to have been the result of the labours of Mr Bowles' gardeners, and it seems, sadly, unlikely that Josiah was involved. There are surely a number of gardens created in the 18th century where enthusiastic amateurs emulated the grander aspects of the great English garden. Mini grandeur is an endearing British gardening trait.

Perhaps Josiah's influence can be sensed and certainly all the right connections are present -. William's first curacy at Donhead, enabling him to be part of the local gentry around Tisbury – perhaps he attended Beckford's Twelfth Night Festival at Fonthill in January 1797 when it would have been quite possible to view the grottoes there. The clerical and legal family contacts of his Shaftesbury family might have allowed him an invitation to Wimborne St Giles and of course his membership of the Bowood social circle enabled him to see Josiah's work there. He clearly enjoyed being part of the Wiltshire gentry, and his interest in gardening must surely have been influenced by the stylish landscapes being created there at that time. Towards the end of his life William moved permanently to Salisbury, where he died, probably in the Canonry, in 1850 aged 88, his wife having predeceased him.

The present owners of Bremhill Court have restored and looked after the Rev. Bowles' house and garden. The house is still a delightful example of an 18th century Rectory, with its elegant Strawberry Hill Gothick windows, pinnacles and turrets. The spacious terrace, sloping lawns and mature trees frame the lake, and from the terrace the view sweeps down and across the Wiltshire countryside towards the Bowood obelisk on the skyline. The standing stones and gentle cascade remind us of William Bowles' interests, reflecting what must have been a wonderfully pleasant, privileged way of life.

24

THE FINAL FLOURISH — NORBITON PLACE

In about 1819 Josiah was requested to build another grotto in Surrey and this was to be his last. He was by then quite old to be shifting heavy stones; he was 66 years old. He must have had help and the logical assistants would have been the Burtons, both stonemasons. The three craftsmen could by this date have travelled to Norbiton Place, just north of Kingston upon Thames in Surrey, by the stagecoach service, which ran from Exeter, through Salisbury, Basingstoke, Andover, Guildford, and on through Esher up to London. As the coach bounced up the great turnpike road, it passed through Cobham, so no doubt Josiah took the opportunity to tell the Burtons about working at Painshill with his father. A coach journey would have cost quite a bit of money, but Josiah had been well paid for his previous work and as he was older he would have been glad not to ride for long distances each day for two or three days. Travellers could ride on the roof, which was cheaper although staying overnight in a coaching inn and having to eat dinner there would have been expensive for even well paid craftsmen. The service was a good one, 24 coaches a week now passed through Salisbury on the Exeter-London run, although when the railways arrived this service became obsolete.

Norbiton Place had become the property of Charles Nicholas Pallmer on his marriage in 1808 to Maria Francis (she had inherited it from her parents). Pallmer was a Jamaican-born plantation and slave owner, so he may well have heard of Josiah through Barnard Dickenson at Bowden Park, another plantation and slave owner. Pallmer became an active MP for Surrey, often speaking for the West Indian interests and chairing the West India Planters' and Merchants Standing Committees. Like many rich men, he spoke on behalf of his own specific financial interests – sugar imports and shipping trades for example - but he also spoke up for improvement to prisons, the need for moral reform of prisoners, and the regulation of lunatic asylums, but presumably against taking any further action to abolish slavery entirely.[1] The Slave Trade Act, having been introduced by Charles James Fox, when he was Foreign Secretary, was passed in 1807 and forbade the trading of slaves in the British Empire, but had not abolished slavery itself. However the Act must have had a financial effect upon the slave owners of the West Indies, and although Pallmer boasted that 1,000 of his plantation slaves had converted to Christianity, they probably had little choice, since he was their absolute owner.

Pallmer, in 1819, still had enough capital and sufficient income to extend the Norbiton Place estate to 300 acres – an arable, sheep and dairy farm, pleasure grounds, kitchen garden, grapery, a nice new grotto and 'other adjuncts of an attractive character'. Sadly none of these delights remain – the site is now part of built-up suburban Kingston-upon-Thames, with a Victorian Gothic church on the site (designed by Gilbert Scott, built in 1868) taking up centre stage. Perhaps the grotto still exists somewhere in a suburban garden, or beneath the adjacent supermarket car park.

In 1828 George Frederick Prosser writes about the grotto in his book *Select Illustrations of the County of Surrey: Comprising . . . Views of the seats of the Nobility and Gentry, with descriptions*[2]

> The fantastic freaks of nature have been happily imitated in the construction of a grotto, which, though unfinished, may vie with most erections of its kind. It comprises a bath, with compartments, and is a good representation of natural rockwork.

The roof pendants are extremely well managed, in imitation of those natural petrifactions called Stallactites, which adorn the caverns of nature. From an elevated seat a view of the whole grotto is obtained, with water issuing from the numerous interstices in its side, and ivy with other creeping plants, in all the wild profusion of nature growing over it. The whole effect is considerably heightened by the retired and sombre air which pervades the place. Near the grotto a very handsome stone bridge, of a peculiarly elegant ellipse, is thrown over a branch of the water before alluded to and which supplies the bath in the grotto

This describes a grotto very similar to the Lanes' previous work and seems with its stalactites, to be a last revival of their more decorative style, particularly that of Painshill and Oatlands Park. Unfortunately no drawing survives. It is easy to imagine Josiah passing on to the Burtons all his accumulated expertise. Uselessly, as the fashion of grottoes had passed and a new style of gardening would not require this sort of craftsmanship.

Gardening writer and guru John Claudius Loudon wrote of Josiah that 'he was perfectly ignorant, but certainly had a genius for this kind of construction. He used to do all the work with his own two hands'.[3] Those hands, his back and his knees must by this stage have been suffering.

The effects of the abolition of the slave trade together with the reduction in sugar revenues as other tropical countries developed their own sugar trade, were becoming a problem for the merchant traders of the West Indies, who previously held a virtual monopoly on the provision of sugar to Britain. Charles Pallmer was certainly affected, as was the seemingly invincibly rich William Beckford. Indeed, in 1822, with his income rapidly declining, Beckford decided to sell the Fonthill Estate. He opened up the Abbey to public inspection with a view to obtaining a better price for his treasures and the furnishings. After selling the Abbey to Mr Farquhar, Beckford decamped to Bath, where he bought two adjacent houses in Lansdown Crescent, linking them by a bridge designed by by his new architect, Mr Goodridge. At the same time he bought the farmland behind the Crescent, up to the top of Lansdown and created a linear park surrounded by wildflower meadows and natural hedges. The linear park would lead to a new Beckford Tower with views across Bath.

Fonthill Splendens was by now reduced to one pavilion and sold first to a Mr Mortimer whose nephew built a woollen mill at the southern end of the lake, employing workers mainly from Warminster to run it, until that failed in 1829. Mortimer then sold Fonthill Splendens and the rest of the Northern part of the estate to Mr James Morrison.

Josiah's links and access to Fonthill were now finally severed. He could no longer walk over to the quarry which had played such a large part in his family's working life, nor was he needed to improve the grottoes any further.

Charles Pallmer survived financially until 1830, when he resigned from Parliament, giving the state of his health as his reason. Early the following year he disappeared, leaving huge debts, including some to his closest friends and colleagues. He was declared bankrupt on 26th April 1831, where in his petition he is referred to as a ship owner, dealer and chapman. There was an overall debt of some £100,000.[4] It would seem unlikely that a mere grotto builder would have been paid for his work, and as the grotto was reported as 'unfinished' in 1828, Josiah and the Burtons had presumably returned home, probably without being paid.

Josiah's sister Deborah had died in Wylye, in 1826 and the final blow for Josiah came in February 1832.[5] His last child, his daughter Tabitha, had left Tisbury to work in London, perhaps in service. She died in the parish of St James, Westminster, aged 31 and unmarried.[6] Josiah was now 78, a tired, probably physically frail old man, embittered at the lack of payment for his last work, and with no children left to look after him.

25

IN WHICH MR LANE MEETS HIS MAKER

Josiah has wandered off again. It is cold in the cottage so he goes outside to look for his wife. She can re-light the fire. She's not in the garden, so he goes through the gate. Standing in the road, he looks up and down for a while, then still in his shirt and breeches but no jacket, he sets off down the road. He has suddenly decided to see his youngest sister Rebekah. The air is very still, and the sky a curious yellow colour. It is going to snow. Although he is now 79 Josiah can still walk well. He is however quite tired when he reaches Jerrards Farm House in Fonthill Gifford and will be glad to get inside. The first flakes start to fall as he knocks on the door. It is opened by a young man who says

'Hello Joss, sorry, Mr Lane. She's not here you know'

This is the third time in as many months that Josiah has arrived on Martin's doorstep looking for his sister.

'She went away a long time ago'

Josiah's legs suddenly give way and he half falls into the arms of the young man, who leads him into the warm living room. Martin, the young man, explains again that Rebekah and Stephen don't live here any more, gives Josiah a mug of hot broth and goes outside to harness the horse up to the cart so that he can take Josiah home. The snow is falling quite heavily by now, covering the white carpet of early snowdrops that line the banks below the old Fonthill boundary walls. Although Martin has wrapped a warm blanket around Josiah, the old man is shivering before they reach his cottage, which is, certainly, very cold inside – dirty mugs, spoons and plates litter the table and the ashes in the fireplace are very dead indeed. Martin relights the fire, settles Josiah beside it and realises he has to get some help for Josiah. He walks down the road to the next cottage.

Deborah Burton and her father-in-law are inside so Martin tells them what has happened. He says that Josiah needs to be looked after – at which Deborah bursts into tears and tells him to mind his own business, she has been doing her best. Her father-in-law explains that they have indeed been trying to help, but Uncle Joss has rejected this, shouting at Deborah that he doesn't know her, doesn't want the food she takes in for him and wants his wife to cook his meals. Or if not Rebekah, then where are Tabitha and Joseph? Deborah has tried to tell him that she is his niece, but he doesn't believe her and has knocked over the soup and tried to hit out at her. She says she's not going in there again, he's a nasty old man.

John Burton is embarrassed. He understands that Joss is disturbed and getting worse. What can they do? After all, they live in a house owned by Joss and he has been a good friend and uncle until a few months ago - when he got the news of his daughter's death – that's when he changed. He's always been a quiet sort of chap says John, but now he shouts a lot and bangs things around. He's angry all the time.

Martin and John decide that they need advice. The two of them go back to Dowdings Cottage, where the newly lit fire is already going out, as Josiah is simply sitting staring at it, still shivering. They persuade him to go to his bed and in the morning John walks down into the village to see Mr William Turner, a big jolly man, whose family have been involved in the community for years. He is a Parish Officer and in turn goes to see the Vicar, Mr Webber, for advice. They decide that Josiah be temporarily admitted to the parish workhouse while they try to find a good woman to move into his cottage to look after him. He should be able to pay for this, they reason, as he has earned very well in the past.

John returns home to tell his daughter in law the news and then goes next door to find that Josiah has got up but is coughing and wheezing. He is sitting wrapped in Martin's old Beckford blanket, but has had nothing to eat or drink. At least, thinks John, he's going to be fed in the workhouse and then we can start to make life manageable for him.

'Where's Rebekah?' enquires the old man. 'I'm not going anywhere *without her'. John comforts his old employer and friend and assures him he will be near Rebekah. Which is true, of course, because the workhouse is right beside the graveyard of St John's. Unfortunately it's not a very welcoming place either; the men are separated from the women and the facilities are very basic indeed, there being only two privies for about 80 people and the rooms are bare, damp and smelly, with only simple cots in dormitories.*

Luckily Josiah is not put off by this. He had, after all, slept for many years in stable lofts and communal spaces when he was away from home, sharing long tables with other workers. In fact it all seems quite familiar and if he didn't feel so breathless and tired, he might, he feels, enjoy being with other people. Is he here to work he wonders? If so, has anyone discussed what stone will be needed, what timber, fossils, feldspar. He will talk about it in the morning he decides. It is Wednesday, so there is bread, dripping and broth for supper. There isn't a great quantity of food, but many of the men are elderly, and he knows some of them, so although talking is discouraged, he feels quite at home. He is reminded of the first time he worked with his father, somewhere, he remembers, in Dorset. Later, lying in his little hard cot, with Martin's Beckford blanket wrapped around him, he recalls a pretty dairy maid, what was her name? Polly, Molly, something like that. His chest is painful when he lies flat so he puts his boots under the straw palliasse to lift his head up. That's better, he thinks, I can breathe. It's pretty noisy in the dormitory, men snoring and farting and he can hear his own chest wheezing. And the church clock chiming all the hours. Still, lots to do in the morning, find out where the grotto is going to be . . . .

In the morning John Burton and Mr Turner come to tell him the good news – they have found a charming widow to look after him. But Josiah does not wake up. He is with his mother and father, his wife Rebekah and their babies, all his baby sisters, Joseph his son and Tabitha his daughter. They are nearly all next door waiting for him and on the 28th January, in a churchyard blanketed by snow, Josiah is buried near his family.

26

NOT EVERY GROTTO WAS BUILT BY THE LANES

The story of the work and lives of Joseph and Josiah Lane stretches from Joseph's birth in 1717 to Josiah's death in 1833. They were pre-eminent in their craft of grotto-making and decorating but there were, of course, other grottoes built during that long golden Georgian age, which were not Lane creations.

Most of these were simple, pretty, shell grottoes, although some were more ambitious, with complicated tunnels and chambers. The 19th and 20th centuries have not been kind to grottoes, but restoration has now become fashionable and a number of grottoes, particularly the shell or mineral/spar encrusted ones, have once again been made safe and are occasionally viewable.

An early 18th century shell grotto, dug into the 4,000 year old mound at Marlborough, in the grounds of Marlborough College, has been successfully renovated as part of a longer term stabilisation and restoration project for the whole mound. This grotto was created for Lady Hertford, Lady in Waiting to Queen Caroline, wife of George II, in the 1730s, being completed by 1739. This became the dramatic venue for poetry readings by Lady Hertford's favourite poets, James Thomson and the Wiltshire-born Stephen Duck. It has a regular round headed arched entrance, flanked by gothic style windows. There are three pools of water at the outer entrance which reflect light into the shell decorated internal walls, and more water is pumped into and out of a giant clam shell. Lady Hertford had seen and admired Alexander Pope's grotto at Twickenham, but considered her own to be much prettier.[1] It does not seem likely, given its date, that Joseph could have had a hand in building it, as he would have been only seventeen years old in 1734.

The regular round headed, tidy arch features in other grottoes of this early period, such a Marble Hill grotto in Twickenham, designed by Charles Bridgman for Henrietta Howard, and the one at Wilbury House at Newton Tony in Wiltshire, 1710. Wanstead Park's boathouse grotto has similar plain arches, built later in 1764 and designed by William Kent. At Stowe, another early one, 1730 by William Kent, his original neo-classical style grotto became covered by tufa and rockwork, but its arches are again round headed and regular. Carshalton Park's grotto, 1720 for Thomas Scawen by Italian architect Giacomo Leoni, was built over springs feeding the River Wandle and is similar in style but decorated inside with flint, glass pieces, coral and shells, with a marble seashell basin. A later grotto, (still with rounded headed entrance) at Busbridge Lakes, Godalming in Surrey, forms part of a group of follies, caves and a hermitage, one of which was intended to be used as a tomb. The grotto has an internal cartouche of dark glass, with the initials HHT and the date 1810 (Henry Hoare Townsend).

Again in the Surrey area, where the Lanes were working in the mid and later 1700s, Lancelot Brown designed the gardens at Clandon Park, West Clandon, and included a grotto in 1776 which again has a regular round headed entrance arch. At Hampton Court House, Thomas Wright, as part of the landscaping there, designed a most beautiful Shell Grotto sometime between 1757 and 1769. It has a painted ceiling, blue with golden stars, and shell decorated walls. This was sensitively restored in 1986 by Diana Reynell.

All these round headed arched entrances seem to confirm that these grottoes are not the work of, or in the style of, the Lanes. Lane grottoes tend to be entered by a narrow entrance leading through a dark, twisting tunnel ending in chambers looking out through jagged, uneven and teeth-like edged openings, often over water. Ceilings were of their trade mark stalactite formations, or of ammonites, or slender needle like projections and patterned in star formations, rather like Florentine Bargello work. Later Josiah created grottoes with great standing stones, again lacking in any symmetry.

A very fine grotto at Bristol took its owner nearly thirty years to complete. This is Goldney House grotto at Clifton, started for a Quaker shipping merchant Thomas Goldney in 1737. Mr Goldney was also a partner in the Coalbrookdale Iron company and founded a Bristol bank. As a shipping merchant he would have had access to a supply of exotic shells, and he used local fossils and minerals to which he also probably had access from his mining activities. This grotto is an ambitious one, with a tunnel leading to a pillar-supported hall – the Lions' Den – with its marble lion and lioness presiding. A narrow cleft leads the visitor upwards, to see on jagged rocks above him, a reclining figure of Neptune, whose arms rests upon a jar from which water flows and tumbles down to two giant clams. A steam pump provided the power. This grotto has all the features that a gentleman could require in his grotto.

One or two of the larger 18th century grottoes were labyrinthine in form, such as the frightening and elaborate Hawkstone grotto in Shropshire. Its silent, pitch black tunnel is 30 yards in length, leading to internal chambers, a labyrinth and a grotto. Through an exit from the grotto chamber the visitor finds himself on the edge of a terrace with a disconcerting sheer drop into the woodland below. The internal labyrinth chamber is 80' x 25' in size, and is supported by smooth pillars carved from the red sandstone rock. This grotto is part of a group of follies and it sits in a wonderful Shropshire landscaped park, created by Sir Richard Hill in the late 1700s.

Scott's grotto at Ware in Hertfordshire has a very complicated and elaborate subterranean series of tunnels and chambers. John Scott was also a Quaker, and a poet. In the mid 1700s he tunnelled into the hillside, the grotto being entered through a classical style porch, with a central arched doorway and side niches. Essentially the grotto is a series of circular chambers, shell lined and linked by long tunnels.

Another tunnelled shell grotto is the one at Margate around which myths seem to have grown. It was discovered by accident in 1835, but is origin is still uncertain. One sensible suggestion is that the grotto is the work of brothers Austen and George Bowles, local masons, who built it in 1800 and then emigrated to America. However, local myth has it that this grotto is a Mithraic Roman shrine, or was built even earlier than the Roman period. Essentially it is a long tunnel, 104 feet in total, with a chamber or shrine at the end.

Other than Joseph and Josiah, the names of grotto builders in the period are few. Loudon, in his periodical *The Gardener*, in 1829 suggests that Mr Turnbull and Mr Scott were the masons for Ascot Place, but this grotto is so much in the Lane style that Loudon must be mistaken. Loudon is also responsible for suggesting that Painshill, Oatlands and Wimbledon House were built by a man called Bushell. Thomas Bushell did indeed built a grotto in Enstone, Oxfordshire, but this was in the 17th century, not the 18th. Perhaps Loudon was thinking of him. Certainly, garden historians, including the eminent Barbara Jones, attribute Painshill, Oatlands and Wimbledon House to 'the shadowy genius of the Lanes', and there is documentary evidence for their work at these grottoes.

One name that does recur is that of Mr Castles of Marylebone in London. Mr Castles was an entrepreneur, an artist and a business man, who leased one and half acres of land opposite Marylebone Gardens, on the edge of built up London in 1737. Marylebone Gardens was a place of pleasure for Londoners, a place in which to promenade, to eat, drink and listen to the music of musicians like Handel, or Arne, a smaller Ranelagh or Vauxhall Gardens. Here Mr Castles created his 'Great Grotto', an area of small buildings and tents where his shell work decorations could be seen, admired and bought. He charged 2/6d. for entry, and it seems likely that he provided drinks and possibly food, as he is referred to in his Will as a victualler.[1] Mr Castles is the artist responsible for the shell decorations at the Wimborne St Giles grotto, and he also built, or decorated, a grotto for Sir Robert Walpole's gardens at Gordon House in the south west corner of the grounds of the Royal Hospital at Chelsea. Mr Castles died in 1757 and is said to be buried in the churchyard of St Mary le bon. Without his entrepreneurial spirit, his Great Grotto declined in popularity and in 1772, London was expanding, the developers moved in and the Great Grotto ceased to exist. Its name has lingered on the form of Grotto Passage.

Mr Castles' Will is dated 6th February 1757 and was proved almost straight away, on the 15th February of the same year, so it would seem likely that poor Mr Castles died immediately after putting his 'mark' to his Will.[2] This does imply that he could not write, but that does not seem to have stopped him from being successful. He left a number of smallish bequests to friends, and to his two executors, but he was at pains to ensure that his Sister Elizabeth Marla should receive an income of six pounds of year for her lifetime from his estate, and that this should be paid direct to her for her sole use and not to her current or any future husband, which may say something about Mr Marla's behaviour. He left his maidservant Mary Sheard a legacy, and one to his friend Abraham Sampson, an upholsterer of Conduit Street. After his sister's death, the remainder of his money, from 'my leasehold and personal estate' is to be divided between 'Mary Ryan, now living with Frederick Atherton in Bury Street St James's', and his nephew John Castles, coachman, of Dublin. From this information it could be deduced that Mr Castles came from Ireland. Mary Ryan does not seem to be a relative – who was she?

Mr Castles also leaves a bequest to Bernard Young, one of his Executors, of 'ten guineas and my Mahogany Chest of Drawers in the room behind my Barr for his many good services'. This would tie in with his description as a victualler. Mr Castles comes across as a generous, gregarious man and one can imagine him behind his candle lit 'Barr' dispensing drinks, discussing projects for shell decoration with prospective clients and enjoying being part of Georgian society. It is recorded that even the Royal family visited the Great Grotto. If he did come from Ireland, did he learn his shell decorating trade there, where there are a number of shell houses? More research would be interesting, but at this time one can only speculate.

Presumably Joseph and John Castles met when they were both working on the grotto at Wimborne St Giles, as their time there must have overlapped. Mr Castles' designs and ideas could well have influenced Joseph's subsequent work. It would be delightful to think that Joseph visited Mr Castles in his Great Grotto at Marylebone, but sadly this does seem rather unlikely.

Tisbury has one more grotto, which is in the garden of the large, imposing former Vicarage. This is a small circular grotto, set into the huge retaining wall which buttresses the highest part of the site – a plateau on which the Victorian Vicarage is built. There was a previous building on the site but the grotto seems much more likely to have created for the Rev. Francis E Hutchinson who was appointed Vicar of Tisbury in 1858, where he remained the incumbent until 1913. He and his rich wife Elizabeth spent their considerable wealth on works for the village of Tisbury, including changes to the structure of St John's (he removed the musicians' West Gallery, replacing the church music with an organ), taking an interest in the school and its pupils, providing them with better facilities, and no doubt becoming involved with the improvements and changes to the Workhouse which took place during his incumbency. He was an eccentric, rather proud of his sporting abilities – for example he would run home from Salisbury, pronouncing this to be quicker than the carrier. When hurdles were put up in the High Street to corral animals waiting to be admitted to the abattoir, he would request that they remain so that he could hurdle down the High Street, coat-tails flying. Having a grotto in one's garden was therefore not surprising, and would certainly have enhanced his wife's summer garden parties.

The grotto is entered through a regular arch, with no jagged teeth effect. The arch is of vermiculated stone and has a wonderful lion's face as a keystone. Inside, the grotto is circular and domed. The floor has an inset mill stone in the centre, above which, in the dome, is a circular stone roundel rather roughly carved, which might, with some imagination, represent cherubs with wings surrounding the sun. The walls and the rest of the ceiling are of more vermiculate and rough cut stones, no stalactite effects, though they are rough and protruding. In the walls are bands of chipped, shaped flints, with many broken pieces of ammonite, one forming a halo over the lion's head in the entrance arch. It is an imaginative grotto, decorative and delightful and adds to the ambience of the Vicar's lower lawn area.

However, whilst it would be good to think there was a Lane connection or influence, it is very unlike a Lane grotto either early or late, and much more likely to have been the work of one or more of the many stonemasons living and working in Tisbury during the incumbency of the Rev. F E Hutchinson. There were still three working Burton stonemasons at the time the Vicarage was built, (soon after the Vicar was appointed) so any one of them could have worked with Josiah. It is possible therefore, for the extended family to have been involved, but understandably the style has changed.

During the period that the architect Papworth was working at Fonthill, much vermiculated stone was used on the estate, particularly to build the urns for the landing stage of the lake, and the entrance to the Arch from the Fonthill Bishop side. Possibly the Vicar was able to procure some of this stone for his little grotto.

27

THE LAST YEARS

The last years of Josiah's life were marked by sadness and the problems of the approach of old age in a society where poor elderly people had only their immediate family to care for them. He returned home some time in 1810, having finished the work at Belcombe Court, only to lose Rebekah, his 49 year old wife the following year. Four years later his young son Joseph Hambleton Lane died, aged only just fourteen.[1] Fortunately he still then had his daughter Tabitha, the twin sister of young Joseph, who was old enough to go into service and earn some money, but he needed someone to run the cottage whilst he was home in Tisbury. After his last contract at Norbiton Place had ended in the early 1820s, he returned home to Tisbury for good. His daughter Tabitha probably left home at this time, to go into service in London, in St James's Westminster, although she may have left in 1819, when Josiah went to Norbiton Place. Sadly, Tabitha died too, in 1832 and this must have been the final blow for Josiah, who was left completely on his own in his cottage in Hindon Lane.

It is difficult to be precise about which cottage Josiah lived in, but the 'estate' which Joseph left to Josiah in his will, with its 'Cyder Mill, Press, and the Mash Tubb', is definitely referred to in Joseph's Will, as Dowdings. Dowdings comprised land on the eastern side of the Tisbury to Hindon Road, about five acres in extent and numbered 541 and 542 on the 1769 Wardour Estate Map, but 576 on the Tisbury Tithe Map.[2] There

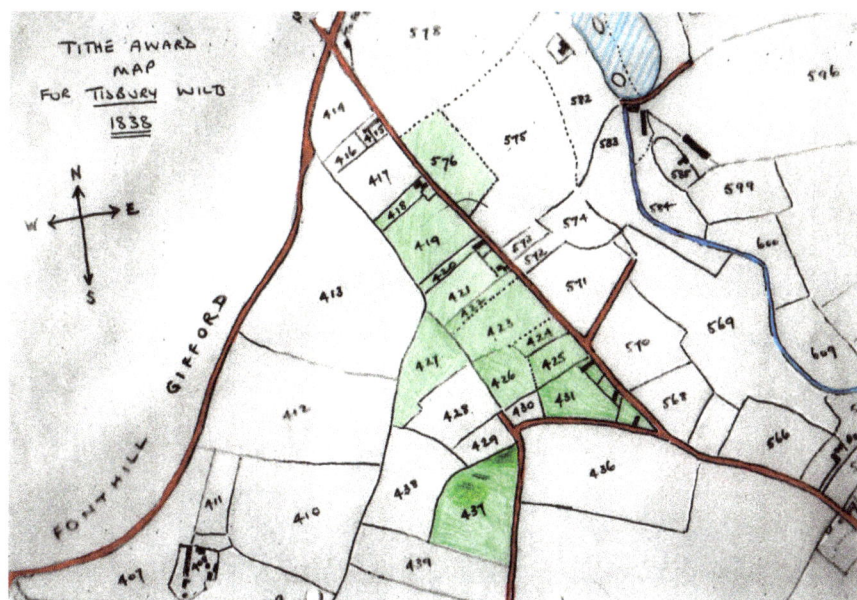

Tisbury Tithe Award Map 1838, showing land owned or rented by the extended family

is no building on this plot. The cottage, garden and orchard must have been across the road, probably plots 418 and 419 on the Tisbury Tithe Award Map of 1838.[3] On plot 420 is a barn (also shown on Andrews & Dury's 1773 map), which seems the most likely building to hold the cyder mill. In 1838, five years after Josiah's death, this house, garden, orchard and outbuildings were in the possession of John Titt, another stonemason, Josiah's nephew and his family, who presumably were given the property by his sister Deborah Titt's family. The land known as Dowdings had, by then, been sold back to the Fonthill estate and was in the possession of the new owner, James Morrison, but farmed by a tenant farmer, James Lampard.[4]

Josiah's niece Deborah, who had married John Burton at Fonthill Gifford church in 1815, lived with her husband as Josiah's very near neighbours in a house with a garden (next to the old barn on plot 420) which by 1838, they owned outright. The Burton family had been listed as Josiah's tenants in 1798 under the records of the Land Tax Redemption Act, so this cottage was almost certainly the property referred to as Josiah's under that Act. They also owned plot 422 outright. They rented a further two acres of called Home ground, plot 421, and ten acres of plot 427, Upper Ground, under a lifehold tenancy from John Thomas Mayne.

LANE FAMILY TREE

Henry Bowles - m - Mary

Walter LANE of Chilmark
d.1748

John Ingram
- m - Mary

Thomas LANE
of Ashley Wood

Sarah Bowles
b.1698 Shaftesbury

George
b.1721

m
on 8.11.1717
at Fonthill Gifford

Mary Flippen - m - (1)
1747

JOSEPH LANE
b.1717 Ashley Wood
Grotto builder d.July 1784

m - (2)
1753

Deborah Ingram
b.1720

Rebecca
b.1759 d.1759

Tabitha
b.1763
d.1763

Rebeckah - m - Stephen Spencer
b.1765 d.? 1781   b.? d.1829?

Josiah
b.May 1787

Isace b.June 1794

Mary Knight - m - John Burton
Stonemason

Joseph Burton b.1799 Farmer
- m -
Anne

Mary
b.1826

William
b.1825

Penny
b.1822

James
b.1821

John b.1818
Stonemason
- m -
Tabitha b.?

Emily
b.1842

Rebekah Mould
b.1762 d.1811

JOSIAH LANE
b.Sept 1753 d.Jan.1833
Grotto builder

m
1794

Deborah - m - Stephen Titt
b.May 1755
d.May 1826 in Wylye

Deborah - m - John Burton b.1792
Stonemason
Son of Joseph

Elizabeth

Deborah
b.1826

Tabitha
b.1799 d.1799

Tabitha
b.May 1801
d. 1832

Deborah
b.1796

James b.1827
Stonemason
- m - Hester

Tabatha
b.1794 d.1794

Joseph Hambleton
b.May 1801
d. Aug 1815

John - m - Ruth
b.1792
Stonemason

Joseph
b.1859

John
b.?

Deborah
b.1777

Stephen
b.1779
- m -
Mary

Robert - m - Lydia
b.? 1821
Yeoman

Robert b.1826

Edwin
b.1855

Lucy - m - Stephen
b.1822
Licensed Victualler
Beckford Arms

Sarah
b.1852

Emily
b.1854

Samuel
b.1856

Stephen
b.1857

Edgar
b.1860

Both these properties paid tithes, Dowdings to the incumbent (vicar) of Compton Chamberlayne, and the Burton's cottage to the vicar of Tisbury and a further sum to the Dean and Chapter of Bristol Diocese for the ten acre field.[5]

Joseph Burton who is listed as a farmer, (John's brother), and other members of the Burton family, also owned land, arable and water meadows including a plot known as Brown's Close. Most of these various pieces of land are all on the west side of the Tisbury to Hindon road, after the small junction, where a lane leads off to the left. Joseph's son William owned plot 423, the arable land known as Bowles Close; a house, garden and orchard (433 and 434, not shown numbered on the Tithe Map but which can probably be identified as the cottages adjacent to the road, opposite plot 570) and arable land plot 437. Father Joseph Burton farmed this land, and lived in and owned plots 431 and 432 and 425 although plot 432 is also not numbered on the Tithe map – this would seem to be the cottage at the very corner of the junction. He also farmed Bowles Close and West Closes, 424, 425 and 426.[6]

It can be seen therefore, that within five years of Josiah's death in 1833, virtually all the land, houses and orchards along the west side of the upper part of Hindon Lane was either owned outright, leased, or tenanted by the extended family of the Lanes, i.e. the Titt and Burton families. Other members of the Burton family owned or rented properties elsewhere in the village, particularly Joseph's sons James, William and Thomas, who had properties along Tisbury Row and including Spilsbury Farm. By 1861 one of Josiah's sister's grandsons owned the Beckford Arms, where he had land, family and servants and is a registered Licensed Victualler.[7]

The Tisbury properties remained in the Lane/Burton/Titt family for many years, but Jerrards in Fonthill Gifford, left to Josiah's sister Rebeckah in 1784[8] by her father Joseph, returned to the ownership of the Fonthill Abbey estate well before 1841, although the Spencers were still in residence there in 1798. There is no further trace of Rebeckah or her husband Stephen Spencer locally. Presumably they left the Tisbury/ Fonthill Gifford area - perhaps for work purposes. A Stephen Spencer aged 55 is recorded as having died in Farnham in Surrey on 18 November 1829, who may have been Rebeckah's husband – that would have been his age in 1829. In the 1841 Census a Josiah Spencer, aged 55 (the age Rebeckah's son would have been in 1841) is listed as living in St Giles in the Fields in London. He is a cabinet maker, with a wife, Martha and two sons, John aged 19 and Charles aged 15.⁹ There is no mention of Isace (or Isaac) Spencer and none of these people can be definitely confirmed as Josiah's relatives.

All of this information about family and properties makes it difficult to understand how Josiah could have ended up dying in the workhouse. In 1836, three years after Josiah had died, the journalist J C Loudon published an article in his *Gardener's Magazine* about the Wardour Castle gardens (Vol. XII p.504). He acknowledges that the grotto there is the work of Josiah, an 'extensive piece of grotto scenery' but adds

> He was a native of the adjoining parish of Tisbury, in the workhouse of which he died last year, at a great age. He was perfectly ignorant, but certainly had a genius for this kind of construction. He used to do all the work with his own hands, and be paid at the rate of about two guineas a week; but, like other money-getting men with ill-regulated minds, he never thought of making provision for age.

Josiah may indeed have been academically 'perfectly ignorant' but the facts are that he had both inherited and bought property in Tisbury and Fonthill Gifford and also owned the Wylye property in which his sister Deborah Titt lived. He must have felt quite secure as far as his old age was concerned, although there is no record of him making a Will. So why did he die in the workhouse?

The old Tisbury workhouse, situated in Church Street beside the Parish Church of St John the Baptist, was built following the 1723 Act which authorised Overseers of the Poor and Churchwardens to purchase or hire buildings for the lodging, keeping, maintaining and employing the poor. These were notoriously unpleasant places and in 1783 George Crabbe wrote in his poem The Village about the terrible conditions and the people who suffered in the workhouses. After mentioning the children, forsaken wives, dejected widows and mothers never wed, he refers to 'crippled age, the lame, the blind, and, far the happiest they, the moping idiot and the madman gay'. So there was an acceptance that this was where disturbed and deserted members of the parish had to go, if there was no-one to look after them.

It seems clear then, that people with mental illnesses were admitted to the workhouse and quite reasonable to suggest that Josiah, who had suffered the loss of all his children and his wife, plus feeling anger and bitterness at not being paid for his last work at Norbiton Place, might well have suffered from severe depression and even dementia. This could well have given rise to the 'ill-regulated mind' comment. The family could not now manage Josiah in his own home and lack of understanding would have caused severe stress for the wider family. Perhaps the presence of the Cyder Press had some effect, as It would be very understandable if Josiah's consumption of his own cyder had become greater. There were not many enjoyable moments left in each day, and the daily mug of cyder might have become two or more mugs. Inebriation was quite usual and acceptable in the period.

Tisbury Workhouse was first recorded as being in existence in 1733. In 1776 the sum of £593 was spent on the poor of the parish, including out-relief and by 1803 this had risen to £1,522, being £310 for the 47 poor people resident in the workhouse and £1,212 for occasional relief for 80 adults and 104 children. This was for a Parish of 2,000 people, i.e. over ten per cent of Tisbury's population were so poor that they needed relief.[10]

In 1816 the Parish adopted Gilbert's Act and appointed two salaried Workhouse Governors. By 1817 the effects of the post Napoleonic Wars had bitten and costs rose to £3,546, reaching a peak of £4,000 in 1818. These figures are taken from the Poor Rate Returns for 1816-21, held in Wiltshire Record Office.

Costs dropped back in the 1820s, by which time there were three Overseers covering the three Tithings of Tisbury, Hatch, and Staple with Chicksgrove. The three Poor Law Parishes of East Tisbury, West Tisbury and Wardour, into which Tisbury was divided in 1835, corresponded roughly to the above three Tithings, each being served by an Overseer. All three parishes joined Tisbury Poor Law Union on its creation in 1835, shortly after Josiah's death, and the Parish Workhouse in Church Street became known as the Union Workhouse.[11] At the same time, the Poor Law Amendment Act of 1834 abolished outdoor relief, creating a greater demand for residential relief, and putting even greater pressure on the inadequate resources of the Church Street building.

Conditions in the workhouse were bad, very basic indeed, and got worse later, and there was, until quite recently, an abiding fear of the workhouse which was known locally as 'the dead-house' although the mortuary was in fact situated in an adjacent building. At least there was, by the time Josiah died there, an adequate diet provided (by the standards of the labouring class at that time) and in 1835, a couple of years after Josiah's death, details of the contract given to John Bracher of Tisbury, a local man, to run the workhouse were:

> The contractor John Bracher agrees to take in paupers as following. Under 7 years of age 2 shillings, under 14 years old 2s 2d, over 14 years 2s 4d, over 70 years 2s 6d per head per week, and included in such charges he will see that each has a change of linen once a week, and bed linen once a month, or find soup, firing, candles, and necessary clothing for each after residency 6 months in the house, or pay the rent and every other expense.

With this letter from Edward Clarke, clerk to the Tisbury Guardians, to the Poor Law Commission was a copy of the proposed diet at the workhouse.[12] The Poor Law Commission replied conveying their consent, 'except so far as regards the allowance of beer to the older paupers, which they do not feel justified in sanctioning, unless in the specific cases in which the medical man pronounces it to be necessary for the health of the pauper, ' So the pint of beer originally proposed by Mr Bracher was removed from the published Diet Sheet.

Tisbury Workhouse.

DIETARY

	Bread.	Cheese.	Dripping or Salt Butter.	Beef or Mutton Soup.	Bacon or Beef.	Potatoes and Cabbage
Under 7 years of age.	oz.	oz.	oz.	Pints.	oz.	At Discretion
Sunday	8	1½		1	2	At Discretion
Monday	12	d°.		d°.		
Tuesday	d°.	d°.		d°.		
Wednesday	8	d°.	8	d°.	2	d°.
Thursday	12	d°.		d°.		
Friday	d°.	d°.		d°.		
Saturday	d°.	d°.		d°.		
Under 14 years of age.						
Sunday	12	1½			4	d°.
Monday	15	2				
Tuesday	d°.	d°.				
Wednesday	12	1½	10		4	d°.
Thursday	15	2				
Friday	d°.	d°.				
Saturday	d°.	d°.				
Above 14 years of age.						
Sunday	12	1½			4	d°.
Monday	16	2				
Tuesday	d°.	d°.				
Wednesday	12	1½	10		4	d°.
Thursday	16	2				
Friday	d°.	d°.				
Saturday	d°.	d°.				
Above 70 years of age.						
Sunday	8	1½	4	2	4	d°.
Monday	12	d°.		d°.		
Tuesday	d°.	d°.		d°.		
Wednesday	8	d°.	4	d°.	4	d°.
Thursday	12	d°.		d°.		
Friday	d°.	d°.	4	d°.		
Saturday	d°.	d°.		d°.		

Bastable, Printer, High-Street, Shaftesbury.

Diet sheet for Tisbury Workhouse

The decay of the building continued and by 1862 a Report of the Commissioners in Lunacy stated:

> The building is in a state of extreme dilapidation. There were only two privies, the site adjoined the parish burial ground, seepage from which contaminated the well. The rooms were barely furnished and comfortless and, according to the inmates, swarmed with rats, mice and bugs; in winter water ran down the walls and the lower floors had to be mopped two or three times a day. The only classification in the house consisted of the separation of the sexes. The old and the young, the good and the bad, are associated together at all events, as to taking exercise in the same yards, which are cheerless and in a rough state and very confined. As for dietary, the dinners consisted on Monday, Wednesday and Saturday of bread and cheese, on Tuesday and Thursday of three ounces of bacon and twenty ounces of potatoes, on Sunday of suet dumpling and on Friday of soup and bread.

And in 1866 after a visit, Mr W H T Hawley, the Poor Law Inspector, noted that:

> *Building* – The site is very low and confined, and some time since fever prevailed in the house. The house is in all respects insufficient for the accommodation of the inmates. There are no separate infectious wards, and infectious cases would be received into the body of the house. No separate sick wards are provided for children. The ventilation, light, and drainage are all defective; the water supply is bad, and the sanitary state of the house unsatisfactory.
> *Furniture*- The bedsteads are very old; the beds are stuffed with straw and chaff; the bedding appears to be in fair condition and sufficient. The conveniences for washing are very defective.
> Inmates -There are only two classes, males and females. The aged men are clothed in cloth suits. The able men and boys in cord and fustian suits. The women and girls in cotton print dresses, and the usual underclothing. There is no employment for the men. The women do the household work, and sew. There is no recreation for the inmates.
> *Medical Attendance* – The medical officer finds all the drugs for

the use of the sick inmates.

Nursing – There is no paid nurse; the nursing is performed by the inmates.

Chaplain – There is a chaplain; Divine service is regularly performed. The inmates who are Dissenters attend their own places of worship by special permission.

School – There is a school, but the children are not separated from the adult inmates.

Generally – The workhouse is defective, and inadequate to the purpose for which it is intended in every particular. A new workhouse is now in course of construction.

This new workhouse, on Monmouth Road at the top of the hill, was opened in 1868, and remained there until the early 1960s. It was used during the Second World War to house non-combatants such as conscientious objectors, German Jewish internees and later during the War by American troops and subsequently the Irish Guards. [13] After its demolition some of the distinctive honeycomb leaded light windows were rescued and can be seen in local houses.

The workhouse buildings today

The old Workhouse building in Church Street was rebuilt as The Wiltshire Brewery and by 1889 was owned by the Styring family. It was later bought by Eldridge Pope brewers, closed down and then used as a grist mill, then a craft factory, the Compton Press, Element Books and a brewery again. Its most recent incarnation is as privately owned apartments.

The sad circumstances surrounding the death of Josiah Lane should not in any way detract from the outstanding achievements of father and son. In an era during which workers had little opportunity of improving their lives, even if they worked really hard, Joseph and Josiah achieved a considerable level of success, not only financially, but also artistically. They are now considered as pre-eminent in their craft, their grottoes receiving the attention and admiration of garden historians, restorers and fortunately, owners.

They were, however, extremely lucky in living where they did, i.e. that Joseph was born on the Fonthill Estate and came to the attention of the estate owner, Alderman Beckford, without whom their lives would have been very different. The Alderman, inadvertently perhaps, was the puppet master in the centre of a web of Lane patrons, pulling the strings, enabling through his contacts, the Lane family to pursue their careers as master grotto builders. Joseph probably learned his original stonemasonry skills at the feet of William Privett of Chilmark, who supplied the stone and the workmen for the gardens at Stourhead. But the Alderman, the richest of the Georgian sugar barons, knew and banked with Henry Hoare (Henry the Magnificent), and Beckford became an MP through his contact with the 4th Earl of Shaftesbury, of Wimborne St Giles.

By the middle of the 18th century Joseph had become more than a competent stonemason, he had discovered the pleasure of creation, and could implement his own ideas. He was lucky that his patrons enabled him to develop his own style. His confidence grew as he worked on the cascade and grotto at Loakes Manor for the 3rd Earl of Shelburne, another Beckford colleague. Charles Hamilton, the nephew of Mrs Maria Beckford, encouraged him to create the grotto at Painshill, where the glittering, glamorous crystal grotto displayed all Joseph's artistic ideas to perfection, and where Josiah began to work with his father. Before the completion of the internal decoration at Painshill, Joseph had to work out how to secure his stalactites to the roof and how to embellish them with the jewel like flakes and this he did, with young Josiah, at Castle

Hill. At Claremont Park, where the Lanes worked for the Alderman's acquaintance the 9th Earl of Lincoln, they met Stephen Wright, who became the designer and Estate Manager at Oatlands Park when the Earl became the 2nd Duke of Newcastle. The landowners at Wimbledon House and Norbiton Place were both rich plantation and slave owners so would have been known to the Alderman and his son William.

After Joseph's death, Josiah was recommended for the work at Bowood Park and benefitted from Beckford's friendship with the now elevated 1st Marquis of Lansdowne, formerly 3rd Earl of Shelburne, and also Charles Hamilton. The latter may also have helped to provide him with the contract for St Ann's Hill for Charles James Fox, since Charles James' father Henry Fox was a close friend of Charles Hamilton.

This web of contacts proved to be the framework for the structure of the Lanes' working lives, but however helpful the Alderman's influences were, the work of father and son had to be good enough for the recommendations that prompted each contract. They had to be sound, reliable craftsmen, able to build good, solid structures, but also to have the imagination and understanding which enabled them to handle the extraordinary richly textured internal decoration and provide the exciting bathhouses, gambling dens and twisting passages of the grottoes.

Their lives and careers spanned the whole Georgian period, from the early 1700s to the 1830s and reflect the fashion for the earlier picturesque gardens and the movement to a wild and more natural landscape. Barbara Jones, in her authoritative, all-encompassing book *Follies and Grottoes*, rates the Lanes as 'among the greatest artists of the 18th century'.[14]

Despite this acclamation, father and son remained attached to their home and family in Tisbury, then a remote Wiltshire village, where no main roads disturbed the rural peace and to be a stonemason was a very respectable trade, providing a better standard of living then than that of a simple agricultural worker. The grotto builders are among the very few artisans whose names have come down through history, whose identity is known, and whose work can still be recognised and celebrated. Their contribution to the art of grotto making enabled the Grotto to take its place amongst the Turkish Tents, Chinese bridges, Octagonal Pavilions, Classical Temples, Follies, Obelisks and Towers of that extravagant and delightful achievement, the 18th century English garden.

BIBLIOGRAPHY

Addison, Sir William, 1980, *The Old Roads of England*, Batsford

Batey, Mavis, 1999, *Alexander Pope The Poet and the Landscape*, Barn Elms Publishing

Bettey, J H, 1987, *Rural Life in Wessex 1500-1900*, Alan Sutton Publishing Ltd

Brown, Jane 1999, *The Pursuit of Paradise*, Harper Collins

Casey, Christine , 2017, *Making Magnificence*, Yale University Press

Cobbett, William, 1983 Ed., *Rural Rides*, Penguin Books

Cochrane, C 1969, *The Lost Roads of Wessex*, Pan Books (David & Charles Series)

Dewhurst, Richard, 2003 , *Crosstracks to Hindon*, The Hobnob Press

Drury, Jill and Peter, 2000 Ed., A Tisbury History, Element Books Ltd

Gauci, Perry, 2013, *William Beckford, First Prime Minister of the London Empire*, Yale University Press

Girouard, Mark, 1980 *Life in the English Country House*, Penguin Books

Hammond, J L & Hammond, Barbara, 1987 *The Village Labourer 1760-1832*, Alan Sutton Publishing Ltd

Harris, John, 1979 *A Garden Alphabet*, Edgeworth Press

Hobsbawm, Eric, 1975, *The Age of Revolution 1789-1848*, Weidenfeld & Nicholson

Jackson, Hazelle, 2001, *Shell Houses and Grottoes*, Shire Library

Jones, Barbara, 1953, *Follies and Grottoes*, Constable, London

Light, Alison, 2014 *Common People*, Fig Tree (Penguin)

Miller, Naomi, 1982 *Heavenly Caves*, George Braziller, NY

Mowl, Timothy, 1998, *William Beckford Composing for Mozart*, John Murray

Mowl, Timothy, 2003, *Historic Gardens of Dorset*, Tempus Publishing

Mowl, Timothy, 2004, *Historic Gardens of Wiltshire*, Tempus Publishing

Needham, John E , 2011, *Forests of the Dinosaurs*, The Hobnob Press

Olsen, Kirsten, 1999, *Daily Life in 18th century England*, Greenwood Press, Connecticut

Parker, Matthew, 2011 *The Sugar Barons*, Hutchinson

Parker, Rowland, 1976 *The Common Stream*, Paladin

Porter, Roy, 1991 Ed. *English Society in the 18th century*, Penguin Books

Sawyer, Rex, 1999, *A History of the Parish Church of St John the Baptist, Tisbury*

Sawyer, Rex, 1995, *Tales of a Wiltshire Valley The Nadder*, Alan Sutton Publishing Ltd

Shallcross, Martin, 2017, *Focus on Tisbury 2001-2016*, Martin Shallcross

Symes, Michael 1998 *Fairest Scenes Five Great Surrey Gardens*, Elmbridge Museum Services

Tannahill, Reay, 1988 Ed., *Food in History*, Penguin Books

Thacker, Christopher, 1976, *Masters of the Grotto*, Compton Press, Tisbury

Timperley H W & Brill, Edith, 1965 *Ancient Trackways of Wessex*, Nonsuch Publishing Ltd

Crowley, Douglas, 1987 Ed., *Victoria History of Wiltshire*, vol. 13, Oxford University Press

Wilton, Andrew, 1979, *The Life and Work of JMW Turner*, Academy Editions

Woodforde, John, 1969, *The Truth about Cottages*, Ebenezer Baylis & Son

Papers

Chatel, Laurence, The Mole, the Bat and the Fairy or the Sublime Grottoes of 'Fonthill Splendens' *Beckford Journal* Vol. 5 Spring 1999

Cousins, Mike, The Lanes and their Legacy [Notes and sources for a lecture]

Cousins, Mike, The Landscape at Fonthill

Cousins, Mike, The Grotto, Ascot Place Berkshire; another Lane grotto? *Follies* Summer 2007

Cousins, Michael John, Castles (Master of the Grottos) & the 18th century Grottoes of London *The London Gardener* Vol.18 2013-14

Craft, Adrian, Fonthill Revisited: Rediscovering William Beckford's Subterranean World [History of Art degree dissertation 1996]

McKewan, Colin, Stourhead Lake Project 2005 Report for the Nautical Archaeological Society

Potter, Jennifer, Gardening; Caverns of the Mind *The Independent* 1994

Richard, Mark, Fonthill - an Inspiration [Architecture degree dissertation 1984]

Symes, Michael, The Grotto, 1990

Walker, Andrea, Way Down in the Grotto, 2011

NOTES AND REFERENCES

Abbreviations

NUA NC   Nottingham University Archive: Newcastle Collection
THSA   Tisbury History Society Archive
UKPR   United Kingdom Parish Records
UKWPR   United Kingdom Wills and Probate Records
UAL   University of the Arts London (Central St Martin's)
VCH   Victoria County History Vol. 13, 1987
WSHC   Wiltshire & Swindon History Centre (Chippenham)

Chapter 1 – *Life at Ashley Wood Cottage: Growing and learning*
1   UKPR for Births, Deaths and Marriages
2   Olsen, Kirsten, 1999, *Daily Life in 18th century England*, p.23 , Greenwood Press
3   'Recovering Fonthill' notes for UAL Symposium 2014
4   Olsen, *Daily Life*, p.107
5   VCH
6   Porter, Roy 1982, *English Society in the 18th Century*, p.135 Pelican Books
7   Olsen, *Daily Life*, p. 238
8   Drury, Jill and Peter, 1980, *A Tisbury History*, p.50 Element Books Ltd
9   ibid p.67
10 VCH

Chapter 2 – *Rural Life: "It was the best of times, it was the worst of times"*
1   Hammond JL and B, 1987 *The Village Labourer 1760-1832*, p 31 Alan Sutton Publishing Ltd
2   ibid p.28-30
3   ibid p.28, 29
4   Brown, Jane, 1999 *The Pursuit of Pleasure*,p.148   Harper Collins Ltd
5   VCH
6   Porter, *English Society* p.92
7   ibid p.91
8   ibid p. 117
9   Bettey, JH, 1987 *Rural Life in Wessex 1500-1900*, p. 60 Alan Sutton Publishing Ltd
10 Porter, *English Society* p.221

11 Woodforde, John, 1969 *The Truth about Cottages*, p.5 Ebenezer Baylis & Son
12 Porter, *English Society* p.215

Chapter 3 – *Openings and Opportunities: Stourhead*
1   VCH
2   Stourhead Archive: Ledger of Personal Accounts for Henry Hoare
3   ibid 6 September 1746
4   Will of William Privett 27 December 1744 proved Sarum 8 March 1747 UKWPR
5   Stourhead Project Report 2005, Nautical Archaeological Society p.6
6   ibid. p.8
7   ibid. p.93
8   Miller, Naomi, *Heavenly Caves* p.86, George Braziller
9   ibid, p.87
10 Stourhead Archive: Henry Hoare's Ledger

Chapter 4 – *Grand Tours and Great Grottoes*
1   Burk, Professor Kathleen: 'The Grand Tour of Europe' Transcript of a Lecture 5 April 2005 at Gresham College, London
2   ibid
3   ibid
4   Miller, *Heavenly Caves*, p.9
5   ibid p.13
6   ibid p.57
7   ibid p.64
8   Batey, Mavis 1999 *Alexander Pope The Poet and the Landscape*, p.57 Barn Elms Publishing
9   ibid p.56

Chapter 5 – *Patronage and Progress*
1   Gauci, Perry, 2013 *William Beckford, First Prime Minister of the London Empire*, 35 Yale University Press
2   ibid p.55
3   ibid pp. 52, 53
4   Mowl, Timothy, 2004, *Historic Gardens of Wiltshire*, p.88 Tempus Publishing Ltd
5   Cousins, Michael, *The Landscape at Fonthill*, pp 3-4, See also the painting by Arthur Devis, 'Fonthill House from the North' 1754
6   Gauci *William Beckford*, pp 140, 141
7   WHC UKPR/Tisbury St John the Baptist 812/8/Bonds Diocese of Sarum D1/62
8   UKPR

Chapter 6 – *A Journey to Wimborne St Giles*
1   Gauci, *William Beckford*, pp. 56, 57
2   Mowl, Timothy, 2003 *Historic Gardens of Dorset*, pp 74 and 184 Tempus

Publishing Ltd
3 ibid pp. 72-73

Chapter 7 – *Fonthill Splendens*
1 Gauci, *William Beckford*, p.157
2 ibid pp 141/2
3 ibid p 144
4 Cousins, *The Landscape at Fonthill*, p.9
5 ibid p.9
6 Steer, Maxwell
7 Chatel, Laurent, 'The Mole, The Bat and The Fairy' *Beckford Journal* Vol. 5 Spring 1999
8 Mowl, Timothy, 1998, *William Beckford: Composing for Mozart* John Murray

Chapter 8 – *Meeting Mr Brown*
1 UKPR
2 Britton, John and Brayley, Edward, 1801 *The Beauties of England and Wales ... Vol. 1 Buckinghamshire*, p.366 London: Vernor & Hood
3 Cousins, Mike 'The Grotto, Ascot Place' for *Follies Magazine* Summer 2007

Chapter 9 – *The Changing Village*
1 Drury, *A Tisbury History*, p.67
2 UKPR
3 VCH
4 WHC Abstract of Returns Relative to Expence and Maintenance of the Poor George III 1803 for Tisbury
5 *A History of the Parish Church of St John the Baptist Tisbury* p.5
6 VCH
7 Dewhurst, Richard 2003, *Crosstracks to Hindon*, p.21 The Hobnob Press
8 ibid p.69
9 Olsen *Daily Life*, p.179
10 Cochrane, C 1969 *Lost Roads of Wessex* Pan Books (David & Charles)

Chapter 10 – *Charles Hamilton comes to dinner and Joseph travels to Surrey*
1 Jones, Barbara, 1953, *Follies and Grottoes*, p.39 Constable
2 Symes, Michael, 'The Grotto' a paper on Painshill Grotto p.2
3 Ibid p.1
4 Hammond & Hammond *The Village Labourer*, pp 397,398

Chapter 11 – *At Castle Hill - Evolving a style*
1 Mowl: *Historic Gardens of Dorset*, p.74
2 Bettey, *Rural Life in Wessex*, pp 116-119

Chapter 12 – *Claremont Park*
1 National Trust Guidebook 2000
2 Cousins, *The Landscape at Fonthill*, p.3

3   Symes, Michael, 1998, *Fairest Scenes; Five Great Surrey Gardens*, p.15 Elmbridge Museum Services

Chapter 13 – *Painshill - The Crystal Grotto completed*
1   Gove, Michael, Chairman Painshill Park Trust
2   Potter, Jennifer, 1994 'Gardening; Caverns of the Mind' for the *Independent* newspaper
3   Symes, *The Grotto*, p.1
4   Jones, *Follies and Grottoes*, p.42

Chapter 14 – *A Death in Soho*
1   Gauci, *William Beckford*, p.188
2   ibid p.190
3   ibid p.194
4   Porter, *English Society* p.220
5   Olsen, *Daily Life*, p.198
6   ibid pp 161,

Chapter 16   – *Oatlands Park : Creation and Destruction*
1   NUA: Newcastle Collection: Stephen Wright's Accounts Bundle May & June 1775 Ne.A.635/21/1
2   RIBA Pix Ref.3926
3   NUA:NC Abstract of Acc. of Artificers Works at Oatlands by Stephen Wright 1775
4   NUA:NC Stephen Wright's accounts bundle 1775
5   ibid 1776
6   Casey, Christine 2017 *Making Magnificence*, p. 119 Yale University Press
7   NUA:NC Stephen Wright's bundle 1777
8   Forge, J Lindus , 1950 'The Grotto, Oatlands Park 1178-1948' Surrey Archaeological Collections
9   NUA:NC , Stephen Wright's bundle 1777
10 ibid 1778
11 ibid 1778
12 ibid 1778
13 Forge, J Lindus *The Grotto at Oatlands Park*
14 Joseph Hayden's Second London Notebook November 1791
15 Jones, *Follies and Grottoes*, p.159
16 Miller, *Heavenly Caves*, p.89
17 *Hansard* HC Deb 17.2.48 Vol.447 cc 980-1
18 Welch, Denton, 'The Denton Welch Journal' 28 May 1948

Chapter 17 – *Wimbledon   House, Joseph's death and back to Fonthill*
1   Cousins, *The Grotto Ascot Place*, p.11
2   ibid p.11
3   Abstract of Title of the Wimbledon House Estate: Wimbledon Museum Co.no.LDWIM00056

4   Cousins, *The Landscape at Fonthill*, p.16
5   UKPR/ Tisbury St John the Baptist 812/14
6   WHC UKPR/Tisbury St John the Baptist 812/19, P2/L/279
7   WHC UKPR/Tisbury St John the Baptist
8   Cousins, *The Landscape at Fonthill*, p.17
9   Wiltshire Land Tax Assessments 1780/1832 Quarter Sessions A1/345
10 Cousins, *The Landscape at Fonthill*, p.18
11 Lees-Milnes, James, 1976 *William Beckford*, pp . 2/30 Compton Russell Ltd

Chapter 18 – *Wild Waterfalls – Josiah at Bowood Park*
1   Symes, Michael, 2011 *The English Rococo Garden*, p.13 Shire Library
2   Thacker, Christopher, 1976 *Masters of the Grotto*, p.22 Compton Press Tisbury
3   Cousins, Mike, 'The Cascade & Grotto at Bowood' p 20 *Follies Magazine* Autumn 2004
4   ibid p.19
5   Bowood Archives – Labourers at Bowood 1776-1794 and Bowood Park Accounts 1785-1789
6   Cousins, Mike   'The Cascade at Bowood' p.21
7   Matthews, Shirley *History of Parliament Vol 1715-1754*, Hamilton, Hon. Charles

Chapter 19 – *Taking tea with Charles James Fox at St Anne's Hill*
1   Chertsey Museum.org .fox Mrs Armistead
2   Chertsey Museum.org.fox John Bernard Trotter
3   goodgentlewoman.wordpress.com Elizabeth Armistead
4   Jones, *Follies & Grottoes*, p.395

Chapter 20 – *Standing Stones, Towers and Umbrageous Grots*
1   VCH, Colt-Hoare
2   UKPR
3   UKPR
4   Mowl, *William Beckford*
5   ibid

Chapter 21 – *Icicles at Ascot*
1   Cousins, *The Grotto, Ascot Place*, p.10
2   andreawalkerconservaton.wordpress.com/2011/12/19/way-down-in-the-grotto
3   Jones, *Follies and Grottoes*, p.160

Chapter 22 – *Mr Turner, Bowden Park and Belcombe Court*
1   UKPR/Tisbury St John the Baptist
2   UKPR Wiltshire Land Tax Assessments 1780/1832
3   UKPR and Census Returns 1841, 1851
4   UKPR/Tisbury St John the Baptist

5   Wiltshire Land Tax Assessments 1780/1832
6   UKPR
7   Mowl, *Historic Gardens of Wiltshire*, pp.98-99
8   www.ucl.ac.uk/lbs/person/view/2146638053 Legacies of British Slave-ownership
9   Symes *The English Rococo Garden*, p.67
10 Mowl , *Historic Gardens of Wiltshire*, p 82
11 ibid. p 83

Chapter 24 – *The Final Flourish - Norbiton Place*
1   historyofparliamentonline.org/volume/1820-1832/pallmer-charlesnicholas
2   Prosser, George Frederick, 1828 *Select Illustrations of the County of Surrey comprising Picturesque Views of the Seats of the Nobility and Gentry*, p.13 (London)
3   Loudon, J C, *Gardener's Magazine* vol.15 pp 426-429
4   historyofparliament /charlespallmer
5   UKPR, St Mary's Wylye
6   UKPR, ST James's Piccadilly, London Metropolitan Archives

Chapter 26 – *Not every Grotto was built by the Lanes*
1   Cousins, Michael 'John Castles ('Master of the Grottos') and the Eighteenth Century Grottoes of London' *The London Gardener* Vol. 18 2013/14

Chapter 27 – *TheLast Years*
1   UKPR/Holy Trinity, Fonthill Gifford
2   WHC: Wardour Estate Map 1769
3   Tisbury Tithe Award Map 1838 Tisbury History Society Archive
4   Tisbury Tithe Awards 1838 THSA
5   ibid
6   ibid
7   UK Census Returns 1861
8   UKPR
9   UK Census Returns 1841
10 WHC Abstract of Returns relative to Expence & Maintenance of the Poor George III 1803 for Tisbury
11 Jackson, Ralph H, 'Tisbury Union Workhouse' for THSA
12 Tisbury Workhouse Dietary THSA
13 Jackson, 'Tisbury Union Workhouse' for THSA
14 Jones, *Follies and Grottoes*, p.159

INDEX

This is an index of persons and places. Places are in Wiltshire unless stated. For members of the Lane and related families the genealogical table on p. 178 may also be found useful. Minor places in the Tisbury–Fonthill area are indexed under Tisbury.

Lightning Source UK Ltd.
Milton Keynes UK
UKHW020857061019

351097UK00003B/40/P